Key Moments

Key Moments

Experiences in a Dedicated Life

LIZ MOHN

CROWN
BUSINESS
NEW YORK

Published in the United States by Crown Business,
an imprint of the Crown Publishing Group,
a division of Random House, Inc., New York.

www.crownpublishing.com

CROWN BUSINESS is a trademark and CROWN and the Rising Sun
colophon are registered trademarks of Random House, Inc.

Crown Business books are available at special discounts for bulk
purchases for sales promotions or corporate use. Special editions,
including personalized covers, excerpts of existing books, or
books with corporate logos, can be created in large quantities
for special needs. For more information, contact Premium Sales
at (212) 572-2232 or e-mail specialmarkets@randomhouse.com.

Library of Congress Cataloging-in-Publication Data
Mohn, Liz.
    [Schlüsselmomente. English]
    Key moments / Liz Mohn. — 1st ed.
        p. cm.
    1. Mohn, Liz. 2. Bertelsmann Stiftung (Gütersloh, Germany)
3. Women philanthropists—Germany—Biography.
4. Businesswomen—Germany—Biography. 5. Women
industralists—Germany—Biography. 6. Human services—
Germany. 7. Charities—Germany. I. Title.
HV28.M66A35 2012
361.7'4092—dc23
[B]   2012010422

ISBN 978-0-7704-3601-8
eISBN 978-0-7704-3603-2

PRINTED IN THE UNITED STATES OF AMERICA

Jacket photograph by Karl Lagerfeld

10   9   8   7   6   5   4   3   2   1

FIRST EDITION

I dedicate this book in love and immense gratitude
to my husband, Reinhard Mohn,
with whom I spent more than fifty years.
A great entrepreneur and founder. A visionary philosopher.
For me he was an infinitely affectionate partner.
By his example and with his convictions,
my life was shaped by him: Humanity wins!

Contents

Contents

Preface

I learned a great many things during the conversations I had with my husband, Reinhard Mohn. I consider it a great gift that for more than fifty years we lived together in an ongoing exchange of ideas, and that I am now able to continue his work at Bertelsmann and the Bertelsmann Foundation. I am deeply grateful to my husband for his belief in me.

My life did not always proceed in a linear fashion. In more than forty years of professional experience, I have experienced highs and lows, overcome great obstacles, and learned from my mistakes. Many times I stood before enormous challenges and had to find new ways around them. Small, spontaneous initiatives grew into large human networks, and efforts that began on the local level became international projects. Like clockwork, I have been asked again and again: "How do you do it?"

My answer is in this book.

Since childhood I have been extremely curious. But like many women of my generation, it wasn't until later in life that I could put my abilities to the test and find out which talents I was really born with. I have remained curious, always wanting to learn. I recognized that common sense alone is not enough to face difficult situations or prevent mistakes—just as our instincts are not enough to go on when making major decisions. We must draw from both reason and intuition.

With this book I not only want to pass on my experiences; I want to give readers the courage to take their lives into their hands and follow their own path. Don't give up, even if things get tough, and don't let setbacks get you down.

Last, I want to pass along the most important thing I've learned: Believe in yourself—and you can do anything!

Liz Mohn

Try It—You Can Do It!

Intuition as Opportunity

I've met countless numbers of people over the past decades, and I've always been curious about how they acquired their skills, talents, and abilities, and how they recognized these qualities, especially attributes that were not immediately apparent. My greatest passion has always been to work with others. Whether I'm hiring new employees at Bertelsmann or meeting young people all over the globe, one thing fascinates me: What makes a person unique? How does someone attain inner strength? Why do some of us not only accept life's challenges but use them for personal growth? And last but not least: What does it take for someone to become a leader? And by leader, I don't mean just someone with a high position within a company. Being a leader means leading by example—whether working in an honorary position or managing projects in social, cultural, or other fields.

Of course, having expert knowledge is a must. To be at the top of your profession, you need to have an excellent education as well as substantial professional knowhow. But that's not all. I have met many extraordinarily talented and well-educated people who become insecure when dealing with others, who won't discuss controversial subjects, and who avoid taking a personal stand. In short, they retreat just when it's their time to step up. They don't trust their own instincts, and they won't take a stand. But a keen intellect and proven capabilities are not enough to be successful. We know today that our brain's subconscious can process much more information than our rational, conscious mind can.[1] Contrary to what we in the West have been taught for generations, feelings or intuition do not stand in opposition to intelligence. Rather, they are a type of intelligence.

Until just a few years ago, it was frowned upon for women of my generation to discuss the impact of their feelings on their decision making. If you showed your emotions, you were considered intellectually weak. And if, furthermore, it was a woman who drew on her intuition, her friends and family would humor her, but her colleagues would certainly not take her seriously. For a long time, concepts like "emotional intelligence" and "intuitive judgment" were considered feminine or female-oriented. Any old-school, traditional manager would have just laughed at them.

This has now all changed, with a special impact on the women of my generation. Today we know that qualities like intuition contribute to making a great leader. If we trust our feelings, we can grow as human beings. We can be open to new possibilities, take unexplored paths, develop new ideas, and launch new projects. We can bring individuals together who otherwise would have never met, and tap into unknowable potential. Believing in the power of your own intuition makes way for endless opportunities. I have seen innumerable examples of it.

Of course, intuition isn't everything. Our emotional knowledge still needs an intellectual framework, including professional expertise and analytical thinking—just as intellect without intuition has its limits. Together, however, intellect and intuition are unbeatable. The more I learned to trust my feelings, the more courageous I became. Suddenly I was going forward with projects that I hadn't dared dream of before. These are the opportunities that I want to talk about here, the key to many of my projects and initiatives. At first, I often just had the sense that something needed to be done, and so I would reach for the phone. An idea was born, and then others followed. A spontaneous initiative grew into a network, which many people then joined. An intuitive decision unleashed great creative force—what began small grew big. And yet in today's schools, students' creative potential is still not nurtured nearly as much as rational and academic learning.

Anyone who wants to make changes in our society

needs to step off the well-trodden path. We must dare to try new things. We must question and rethink that which is familiar, to make sure we're really on the right track. We must be allowed to make mistakes. And we must become curious again, to want to learn our whole lives long.

Between Fear and Hope:
A Childhood During Wartime

The world into which I was born was not a safe one. My life began on the eve of Germany's declaration of war on the Soviet Union. The adults were fraught with worry. Today we know that a mother's fear, along with the anxiety and hardship she experiences during the first weeks of her child's life, can have a profound impact on that person's subconscious. As adults, we carry our mothers' worries with us, perhaps for all our lives. But early life lessons are also what made the women of my generation strong. We learned that life is not a cakewalk, and that survival not only demands great strength but can even make you stronger.

The changes in society that we children of the war have witnessed are immense, especially we women, who had to fight hard for our chance at an education and a career, and for a voice in society. For the women of my generation, none of the above were givens. Today, whenever I give a lecture and see so many well-educated young women in the audience, I am overcome with joy. And vice versa: these young women are often astonished at the scope of my duties and my many interests. "How do you do it all?" they ask. "What gave you such strength and courage? What made you the woman you are today?"

What, indeed, makes us who we are? At what point do we discover our personal strengths? How do we unearth our specific talents? And what gives us the courage never to give up, no matter how many setbacks and mistakes we encounter? How do we stay true to ourselves and to the goals that we've set?

It was a long journey from being a little girl from Wiedenbrück to being a head of Bertelsmann AG and the Bertelsmann Foundation. I had the great fortune to be at my husband's side on his many travels and to meet extraordinary personalities from all over the world. These experiences were priceless. They also led to greater self-knowledge. Today I know my strengths and my weaknesses, but most important, I have learned to continually reexamine what I do: Was that the right thing to do? How can I improve? What do I have to change?

In the process of being continually pressured by new challenges and demanding situations, I, like many women, have learned to listen to my inner voice. It wasn't always so. But fortunately, as women's accomplishments in leadership positions have grown, the large role that intuition plays in our daily decision making is getting its due notice.

My personal life and the growth of my professional responsibilities have consistently been marked by turning points. Those were those moments when I knew, *This is it! This is what I want to do! This could be successful!* And more often than not, the only way to achieve success was through hard work, tenacity, discipline, and perseverance. Numerous national and international projects, as well as the different topic areas of the Bertelsmann Foundation, were created this way. Small initiatives grew, pushing forth against all resistance. All this has given me a wealth of experiences that I share in this book.

The two conflicting emotions of fear and hope informed my entire childhood. Because Wiedenbrück, where I was born, is very close to the Ruhrgebiet and to Bielefeld, we experienced heavy bombing. Countless times my mother grabbed me from my childhood bed and carried me to a bomb shelter. Those years of fear, hunger, cold, and hardship are seared into my memory. But even in the darkest hours, my mother was there, reaching for me. I cannot praise her optimism and courage enough.

My father had many serious health problems. As an invalid, he was not drafted, but for a man of his generation, this was a grave dishonor. He suffered greatly. As the second of five children, I saw how, during this difficult time of war, my mother raised us mostly by herself.

She had no choice but to make all decisions and take responsibility for caring for her family. She often sang to us while she cleaned, cooked, and sewed, and it's from her that I learned so many songs.

Although we had to count every penny, my mother never let that stop her from being kind and generous to others in need. Nobody ever left our home without a bowl of soup or a piece of bread. During the darkest years, my mother got much of her strength from her Catholic faith. We children, too, were in church every morning at seven before the start of school, and of course we said our prayers before each meal.

My mother never complained. She took what life handed her and, with her love of life, made the impossible possible for us children. Not until decades later did I realize how much her strong personality and gregarious and joyful nature shaped my own character. Back then, she was everything to me. I clung to her and never wanted to let her go. I fought tooth and nail against going to kindergarten, although was no escaping the first day of school. I was terrified! But this first step into school also made me curious, and I soon got used to my classes.

When I felt safe and loved, my confidence and courage grew. I forgot all my fears and simply tried the things I wanted to try. At one point I walked all by myself along the banks of the Ems River. I had decided that I wanted to listen to the birds. Later, horrified neighbors reported to my mother that, starting at four years old, I tried again and again to jump into the river to make my way along the reeds to the other side. I wanted desperately to learn how to swim, and I did. Since then water has been my element, and I have always been an enthusiastic swimmer. As young as I was, I had discovered the strength of my will. My mother barely recognized her formerly frightened little girl, and she had the feeling that there would be quite a few surprises in store for her.

I took every opportunity to test my new self-confidence in school and gym class. "Try it. You can do it!" Encouraged by my teacher's rallying cry, I was the only student in my class who dared to jump off a five-meter diving platform. *You can do it,* I said to myself, as my knees shook and my heart was beating in my throat. These words have now become my motto.

Bit by bit, my courage and my love of adventure grew. Before long, my mother could barely contain me. At the age of six, I joined the Girl Scouts. I became a "Wichtel" (Brownie) and stayed a member for many years. I loved our lengthy excursions into nature and our trips to youth hostels, as well as singing and hiking together. I learned to be responsible for a group and to defer my own wishes to the good of the community. These early experiences had a great impact on me, and they opened me up to the possibilities that can evolve from an organization that is led with a social conscience.

Over the years, I became a real bookworm. I loved every classic young adult novel that I could borrow and was especially taken by adventure stories. I was a good student in history and German but wasn't a big fan of math. And even though I got along fine in school, when I was fourteen, I had to admit to myself that I wouldn't be admitted to a school of higher education.

I Wanted to Do More with My Life

Once school ended, I didn't know what to do with myself, so I planned a bicycle trip with my cousin. My father asked a truck driver to give us a ride to Würzburg, and from there we would bike back to Wiedenbrück. But on the way back, we came across a road sign for the pretty little town of Rothenburg ob der Tauber, and from there we followed signs to Munich. We were constantly coming up with new destinations. It was a gorgeous summer, and we had seen very little of the world. We drifted along, getting rides from truck drivers along the way, and ended up traveling from the Bavarian lakes in the south all the way to the North Sea island of Helgoland. I still remember the ache I felt when we came across a group of young students. I could sense their lightheartedness and the endless possibilities that lay in store for them. The future was theirs for the taking. I didn't have that kind of freedom.

While I was away, my mother found an apprenticeship for me to train as a dental assistant—in those days, this was considered a stroke of luck. But I wanted to do more with my life, and I kept my eyes open for people who could help me. An acquaintance of mine who worked at Bertelsmann was always telling me about all the wonderful opportunities there. Why didn't I give it a try? Without telling my mother, I applied for a position at the distribution center of the Bertelsmann Book Club, and I got hired. I had no idea how much this would change my life.

As a young Catholic-raised woman, I had to follow strict rules, including not going out alone at night. Six weeks after I began working at Bertelsmann, I was invited to the annual company party. I begged and pleaded with my parents until they finally gave me permission to go—though neither of them was especially thrilled, since the legal age at that time was twenty-one. After much deliberation, they finally permitted me to stay out until ten o'clock at night. This night would change my destiny.

Along with other young apprentices, I watched Reinhard Mohn, the head of Bertelsmann, enter the room, accompanied by a group of colleagues. We were all very curious about him—he was a good-looking young man whose ideas were widely discussed in the company. His straightforward and confident manner made an impression on me, and it seems that he noticed me as well. Of all the girls in the room, I was the only one he asked to dance. I was touched by his openness and his charisma. Someone took a picture of us as we fought for the last remaining chair in a game of musical chairs. He won.

An Uphill Road

The years that followed were not easy. I very much enjoyed working with so many different people at Bertelsmann, but the man I loved was unavailable. Reinhard Mohn got married and started a family right after the war. He was one of the many men whose youth was stolen by the war, and who only afterward discovered life's joys. Fate had brought us together, but in the late 1950s divorce was out of the question. We had three children together, born in the 1960s: Brigitte in 1964, Christoph in 1965, and Andreas in 1968. Reinhard Mohn tried to spend as much time as he could with us, but the chance of our having a life together was slim. During this time, my future husband wrote me a letter every day. Long after we were married, he organized those letters into binders. It became a collection of quite a few binders, which contain our worries but also our hopes and dreams of that time. I still find it difficult to look through them. It was not an easy time, but I'm very grateful that we could go through it together.

While my life as a young mother was very fulfilling,

it came with a new set of fears and worries. Our daughter, Brigitte, became very sick with severe asthma when she was just four months old. For years her doctors and I fought for her life, and I endured sleepless nights, hours of terror, and moments of desperation at my little girl's side. As I watched her suffer, I developed a more critical viewpoint toward the Catholicism of my youth, and I began to gain confidence in the power of my own strength of will. A mother who has spent so many years living in fear for her sick child either breaks down or recognizes that in her darkest hours of hopelessness and need, she can gain unknown strengths that help her continue down her path.

During this time my children and I had to overcome a number of other serious health setbacks. While this can put a severe strain on any relationship, it only brought my husband and me closer together. We learned to talk about even the most difficult and painful things. One of the most important prerequisites for having a successful relationship is to speak candidly with each other, and I consider it a great gift that my husband and I were able to have such an open exchange of ideas. I learned a lot from him, but he, too, greatly valued my intuition and my sincere and spontaneous exchanges with others.

When he was with our children, my husband became a child himself. He enchanted Gitte, Chris, and Andreas with his humor and imagination. For the children, he was their beloved "Tata," who concocted practical jokes with them and told them elaborate, made-up stories. When it came to raising a family, we fully agreed on the important principles. We wanted our children to remain down to earth and to treat everybody politely and with respect. We worked hard to instill in them the value of responsibility and fairness when dealing with others. And while we were always open to discussion, we also set boundaries when a debate had no end in sight.

As the children got older, my husband told them more about his work and the needs of his company. For a passionate entrepreneur like Reinhard Mohn, there was no such thing as leaving work behind in the office. Even in his free time he thought about the company's growth and the changes to the corporate culture that he wanted to implement with his coworkers. His work fulfilled him.

In the 1960s and 1970s it was still fairly common for women to fully dedicate themselves to housework and child rearing, if financially feasible. But more often than not whenever my husband spoke with such enthusiasm about his work, I felt a pang of longing. I, too, wanted challenging work and a position of communal responsibility. And as our children grew older, they clearly needed my presence less and less.

My first corporate undertaking grew out of my own life experiences. Reinhard Mohn was twenty years older than me and a hard-working businessman. He was also a deeply philosophical man, who examined everything he did and who invited me to take part in his critical thinking. There is no doubt: he was my teacher, and he gave me insight into politics and society, morality and ethics, and management and leadership principles. His analytical skills were impressive, and I was his eager student. But with time I learned to ask questions and to point out concepts that seemed incomplete or even erroneous to me. What was once a monologue became a dialogue, a mutual give-and-take. I now recognized problems, found gaps within existing structures, and saw where remedial action was needed. "Why don't you give it a try?" my husband would say. And so I did.

One of my first initiatives, somewhat reflective of the time, was the establishment of the Bertelsmann Women's Circle, which would give the wives of the Bertelsmann leadership insight into their husbands' work. Over the years, the Women's Circle grew from offering lectures and academic trips to creating social aid projects and other initiatives.[2] Quite a few Women's Circle volunteers were able to turn their passion into their profession and became indispensable employees of the Bertelsmann Foundation.

My husband presented me with another project: overseeing the construction of Bertelsmann's headquarters, slated for completion in 1976. Dissatisfied with the architect's initial designs, he asked for my help. The planning phase lasted for over a year, during which time I strongly advocated opening up the interior of the building to achieve transparency and clarity. (To this day, those qualities distinguish our Gütersloh headquarters.) My husband was extremely satisfied with the result. He was impressed that I stood behind my work 200 percent. And he was very aware of how much my enthusiasm grew when I was developing my own ideas.

Spontaneity and Intuition: First Experiences While Developing the Bertelsmann Foundation

In 1977 my husband established the Bertelsmann Foundation, and I quickly became very much involved.[3] We spent many hours talking about why he started it. On the one hand, he wanted to ensure the fiscal continuity of Bertelsmann AG by eventually taking over the assets of the Mohn family and guaranteeing the company's financing. On the other hand, he firmly believed that our society's democratic way of life was subject to ongoing revision and improvement. He wanted very much to utilize his experience in corporate culture to propagate the principles and uphold the development of a democratic state, via the foundation's wide reach.

The Bertelsmann Foundation was designed to be a conceptual as well as a functional body that would work with specialists and with public and private institutions to develop its projects.[4] In its early years, it was made up of a close-knit group. In 1979 Hans-Dieter Weger became its first hired employee. As director of the foundation, he worked very closely with my husband to develop its first initiatives.

Watching the foundation grow inspired me hugely, as did meeting so many scientists, politicians, artists, and various ambassadors of culture. On numerous trips with my husband, both within Germany and abroad, I was introduced to many shades of critical thinking and witnessed many controversial yet also constructive debates. When I think back on this time, I realize that these were the years of my true education. My many conversations with my husband, and with so many diverse personalities, gave me access to an immense realm of subjects. I couldn't have wished for a more thorough course of study.

Learning gave me a charge, and I could barely contain my thirst for knowledge. I was an avid listener and gradually began to ask questions. I soon developed a great affinity for discourse and was happy to discover that my own judgment was often spot-on. My husband took note of the strength of my intuition and found it to be an ideal counterpart to his own analytical way of thinking. Fortunately, he fully supported my interest in people and in sociopolitical issues. Recent research into the human brain has only confirmed what I experienced: a belief in one's own capacity for intellectual growth is imperative to reaching one's full potential. Many people who are aware of their inherent aptitude won't take advantage of all their capabilities. They simply come to a standstill after completing their education, satisfied with all they have learned. Only when we believe in the limitlessness of our potential are we able to move on to the next level, to go beyond our boundaries, to learn from our mistakes.

If there was something I did not know, I would not rest until I found someone who could answer my question. Every new issue I was confronted with became an educational journey, because each conversation with an authority raised new queries. Learning is a process with no beginning, middle, or end; it is life itself. I was fortunate to discover that learning makes you happy. And I am fully convinced that the lifelong drive to learn will be one of the most important skills to have in the future.[5]

Having new experiences is a great motivator in itself. Motivation leads to more of the same, and newly learned skills often unveil heretofore unknown talents. Learning leads to character growth, and our quest for knowledge can become our key to happiness. Step by step, project by project, on trips abroad or at home in Gütersloh, I began to line up my responsibilities. I initiated many social, cultural, and medical projects after having conversations with experts, pursuing answers to my personal questions, or simply having the desire to help. Over time, these projects evolved into the main topic areas of the Bertelsmann Foundation.[6]

But my work does not deal merely with big issues. Specific, goal-oriented assistance for those in my immediate surroundings is still very much a part of it. We began providing this type of aid in 1983 by establishing patient libraries in hospitals and old-age homes in the region.[7] Even today I still take the time to personally visit old-age homes, women's shelters, and other social service facilities. There is always room in my calendar for a spontaneous conversation, a kind word, or even a communal sing-along.

My interest in health and medicine continued to give rise to new ideas and set other projects in motion. While my husband spent his free time deep in thought, I reached for the phone. With each new issue that came my way, I first thought about which people to connect with one another—which meeting of the minds would have the greatest impact on any issue. I did, and still do, very much enjoy getting people excited about a new idea and bringing them together to work on a project. During my first years with the Bertelsmann Foundation, I learned that I was quick to see where new initiatives were needed, and that my way of creating connections between people was much more efficient than the traditional route, going through institutions. My various encounters with other cultures and my many meetings with international figures made me very aware of cultural differences among peoples and nations. But I also learned that a simple, inviting gesture can be a stepping-stone toward a deeper connection and mutual understanding.

When my husband saw how easily I approached people and made connections that would have taken much longer to establish using official means, he began to assign me more diplomatic tasks. I very happily took them on. We got married in November 1982, and following my husband's wishes, I increasingly took on official duties at the Bertelsmann Foundation. In 1981 he withdrew from the operating side of Bertelsmann AG, retiring as chairman of the board, and joined the supervisory board. More than ever, he thought about the risks and opportunities inherent in political systems. He was convinced that a nation's strength and performance determine its future generations' quality of life. His own catastrophic experiences during World War II made it clear to him that any development of a civil society without ethics or a legal code would end only in violence and chaos.

We often talked about what the ideal conditions for a prosperous future society would be. Continued growth of international competition, we felt, demanded not only an increase in each citizen's individual contribution but also an ongoing dialogue with other cultures and an awareness of different national, political, ethical, and cultural perspectives. Germany could learn so much from other countries! And vice versa—Germany's research and development across so many disciplines could prove helpful to others.

The Bertelsmann Foundation's corporate structure turned out to be ideal for exploring which nations' initiatives could best be implemented in Germany, and for investigating which of Germany's projects could prove most beneficial to others.

Projects of the Bertelsmann
Foundation and Other Initiatives

Learning Through Dialogue— International Encounters and Seminal Experiences

As Reinhard Mohn was building international relationships for Bertelsmann, he recognized that the best way to overcome historic, national, and cultural differences was to have personal exchanges with others about shared economic and sociopolitical interests. My husband and I spent hours talking about this in our evening conversations! When two people share a common goal, they will have the courage to pursue a mutual understanding. Any dialogue between two cultures can never be based on a one-sided superiority but rather depends on mutual honesty, an understanding of historical events, and the respect for different ways of living.

My husband and I each had our own unique experiences of World War II. As a young soldier, he had fought at the front, only to realize later that an entire generation had sacrificed its youth to an immoral order. I had been a young child, debilitated by the fear and desperation of the adults around me.

We always said that we would do whatever we could to support any and all dialogues and cultural exchanges among nations. I am convinced that in today's world of unforeseeable military threats, this is the only way to secure and maintain peace. There is no substitute for dialogue!

As chairman of the board of Bertelsmann AG, my husband established close ties with Israel. In 1979, one of the first projects the Bertelsmann Foundation initiated under his chairmanship was the establishment of a program of study at the Hebrew University of Jerusalem. The program, which was integrated into the sociology and political science departments, examined the quality of working life.[8]

In 1987, I accompanied my husband to Jerusalem to attend a conference on the future of the publishing industry in the light of existing language barriers.[9] I found the lively discussions there quite moving. I especially wanted to meet Teddy Kollek, the legendary mayor of Jerusalem, about whom I had heard so much. We made an appointment to meet for breakfast. Our very first conversation made a big impression on me. This distinguished man was not only very charismatic, he was a true guardian of the city and its people. Later I found out that he normally had about five breakfast meetings daily—starting at his home and then moving on to various city hotels—during which he met with diverse people to discuss any variety of topics. I later got to know his wife, Tamar, who was just as remarkable as he and fully supported her husband as his steady companion.

Teddy Kollek was able to make great strides for Jerusalem by creating social and cultural initiatives to support the coexistence of different religions. With great care he built schools, libraries, and old-age homes for the Jewish and Arab populations, and he made sure these institutions were respectful of religious interests and cultural identities. The only group that tested his patience were the Orthodox Jews, for he felt their way of life was difficult to integrate into modern Israeli society. But he built special hospitals so that both Muslim and Orthodox Jewish women could undergo breast exams. Breast cancer was widespread at the time in Israel, partially because of religious barriers against preventive breast exams. This kind of thing drove Teddy Kollek crazy, and I greatly admired him for his courage and dedication when it came to such sensitive issues.

Over the years, a real friendship developed among my husband, myself, and Teddy and Tamar Kollek. They visited us in Germany, and quite a few Israeli-German ventures sprang forth from our friendship. One such endeavor is the Computer Studies Center that opened in 1986 at the René Cassin High School in Strasbourg. Run by Everyman's University in Jerusalem, it went on to generate other computer study programs.[10] The Adam

Institute for Democracy and Peace in Jerusalem, founded in 1984, was supported by the Bertelsmann Foundation from 1988 until 2004 and represents one of our longest-running initiatives.[11] Its goal is to teach students between twelve and fifteen the values of democracy and peace as they pertain to the specific situation in Israel. Furthermore, the institute develops appropriate methodologies of education and research. In 1989 the Koteret School of Journalism and Communication was founded in Tel Aviv—the brainchild of my husband and Teddy Kollek.[12]

At my suggestion, in the 1990s the Bertelsmann Foundation moved away from backing individual institutions and toward supporting personal and cultural exchanges between the two countries. In 1992 we initiated funding of the Institute for Studies at the Hebrew University of Jerusalem,[13] which sponsored many conferences and symposia. In 1997 these conferences gave rise to the European-Israeli Network—an academic workshop and exchange program that has since been established in many Israeli secondary schools.

One of our most important projects, one that has always been close to my and my husband's heart, was the creation in 1992 of the German-Jewish Dialogue series.[14] This forum has met with great positive response from key German decision makers and from representatives of the Jewish community. In 1992 we also began supporting the University of Tel Aviv, helping fund its Center for Holocaust Studies,[15] which takes a close look at the effect of the Holocaust on today's societies. As much as we must pay due diligence for our grave history, we must also try to create a shared future. For this reason, in 2000 the Bertelsmann Foundation initiated the German-Israeli Young Leaders Exchange, to facilitate the flow of information and the sharing of experiences among young German and Israeli leaders in a forum where they could meet and network.[16]

After many changes in the political landscape, Europe began facing new challenges. With this in mind, in the fall of 1987 the Bertelsmann Foundation initiated a project called Strategies and Options for the Future of Europe.[17] Europe needs better cooperation among its nations, and more efficient policies, and it must support the progress of its diverse cultures. We must uphold the free societies that have grown out of the European tradition, even as we respect the identities of the culturally diverse nations and cultures.

The main objective of this sizable endowment program was to find out what politically had to be done in Europe, beyond the obvious. In addition, the ever-changing political developments in Eastern Europe raised strategic and sociopolitical questions. We thus formed a study group to further examine the continent in light of all these changes, called Europe's Role in the World.[18]

An early highlight of our project on Europe was the conference "Europe's Future—A Continent's Culture and Constitution," organized by Bertelsmann in October 1990 in Rome. Many international participants were invited to this high-caliber conference, whose goal was to ascertain Europe's political and cultural future. In the months between the conference's initial conceptualization and its opening, much had changed in Europe. Revolutionary changes were transforming the European continent. The Bertelsmann conference had to address these sudden new challenges head-on. The debates centered on the new European framework, and on the issues that arose out of this new paradigm: questions of modernization and innovation, political changes and integration, security, and the new European identity.[19]

A second important event that was part of the Strategies and Options for the Future of Europe project was a conference entitled "The Mediterranean Challenge—and the European Answer." We worked with the Catalonian president Dr. Jordi Pujol i Soley, who hosted the conference in October 1991 in Barcelona. A number of personal encounters during this time made this conference especially memorable to me. About 120 participants came from almost all the Mediterranean countries, as well as from Russia, the United States, and the rest of Europe. Our speakers included, among others, the Italian minister for foreign affairs Gianni De Michelis, the Dutch minister for foreign affairs Pieter Dankert, the former Turkish minister of foreign affairs Vahit Halefoğlu, Crown Prince El Hassan bin Talal of Jordan, and the theologian Hans Küng. The event took place under the patronage of Germany's president, Dr. Richard von Weizsäcker, along with His Majesty Juan Carlos I, King of Spain. Felipe, Prince of Asturias, represented Spain's royal dynasty.

During the conference, two participants from Egypt asked my husband for advice concerning education reform in their country. They had heard a great many things about his engagement for education in Israel. Drawing on our experience as an international media conglomerate and our initiative to build libraries, we decided to build a library in Cairo. To begin with, we had to investigate and define the terms for building the new facility. We were surprised to find out that more than 60 percent of the population of Egypt was illiterate! This shocking figure inspired us even more to break ground on the library project. Education is one of the most important requirements for a free and peaceful world. Only those who find a way out of the cycle of poverty and violence can become responsible citizens. My husband and I were always convinced that helping people to help themselves is the most effective way to aid those in need.

The government of Egypt donated an old villa, situated at the shore of the Nile—it had once belonged to the former vice president Abdel Hakim Amer. The

Bertelsmann Foundation financed the renovations and assisted with staffing and marketing. We held the official opening and dedication of the Giza Public Library on March 21, 1995, in Cairo.[20] Our first large public project, it would become a focus of cultural life in Egypt. Later we opened branches in less prominent locations—smaller libraries, often in the poorer sections of town. The demand was then, as it is now, enormous! Many books become so well thumbed that they need to be replaced every few years.

Among my many friendships, I still feel especially close to Queen Noor of Jordan. We met after the death of her husband in 1998, at an event hosted by the United World College in Berlin, of which she is president. Our first conversation was already quite intimate. She spoke a lot about the special relationship she had with King Hussein, and she invited me to visit her soon in Jordan. I met her half a year later in Amman while my husband and I were traveling in the Middle East. I could see how much she was still suffering from the loss of her husband. It was a difficult time for her, yet her hospitality and her warmth were indefatigable. She had arranged a small, private dinner for me at her palace in Amman and had set the table especially in the library. She wanted to make a special gesture to me as a representative of the Bertelsmann publishing house. She thought of everything and took great care to make sure things were just right. Her entire life had suddenly changed with the death of her husband, yet her warmth, intelligence, and kindness were unforgettable. As we both deeply believe in the values of cultural exchange and global tolerance, we decided to start initiatives that support tolerance and teach strategies for conflict resolution.

Over the years of being involved with cross-cultural relations, I made many new friends and allies in the Arab world. One of my most valued friends is Sheikh Nahyan bin Mubarak Al Nahyan of Abu Dhabi. This modern, well-educated man had studied at Oxford, and whenever he was traveling in Europe for business, he was always on the lookout for new educational initiatives. It was something that he felt his country, for all its riches, still needed.

Sheikh Nahyan was especially intrigued by the library in our hometown, the city of Gütersloh, which the Bertelsmann Foundation had built as a pilot project.[21] Our concept had been that the Gütersloh library would be a meeting place as well as an interactive information and media center. The facility, its organization, and its cost-effectiveness have made this library an international benchmark. Sheikh Nahyan was looking for ways to connect his country's libraries and universities in a similar network. He also modernized many aspects of secondary education in his country. He implemented smaller units of study in the universities and directly connected students to experts in the field—innovative alternatives to the massive institutes of learning such as we have in Germany. Especially impressive, two-thirds of all students in Bahrain, Qatar, Kuwait, and the United Arab Emirates are women, and in Oman and Saudi Arabia more than 50 percent of those enrolled in universities are women. Women's universities like the Zayed University in Abu Dhabi and Dubai are expanding quickly. Without a doubt, the large proportion of female students reflects women's changing role in society and their desire to contribute to the workforce. All these women are hoping that in the course of their studies, the job market will open up for them.

Sheikh Nahyan bin Mubarak is an extraordinary man not only in education reform but in private. Whenever I am in Abu Dhabi, he welcomes me with immensely generous gestures of hospitality. Through him, I have gained great insight into the complexities of Arab culture.

In all my discussions, especially with younger people, and on all the trips I've taken, I've always noticed how important it is for people from different cultures and countries to exchange ideas and get to know one another. More than anything, the expansive globalization that began in the 1980s has raised a lot of questions: How will globalization change our society? Is the much-discussed "clash of civilizations"[22] really unavoidable? What challenges lie in our future, and how can we best deal with them? Is it possible for a region to follow the trend of increasing globalization yet still retain its cultural identity? Neither our leading heads of state nor the world's big economic players, I realized, had any real answers to these questions.

Today, anybody in a position of responsibility is going through a learning process. We all must assess how to meet new challenges, come up with new ways for different cultures to coexist, and advocate mutual respect and tolerance.

With the rise of the new media in the 1990s, the whole world can now be connected within seconds. What does this mean for our political systems? How can we best manage this wealth of information? How does this information influence the thinking and political awareness of our youth? Are we fully aware of our responsibilities? And what will our common goals be in the future?

These types of questions are always going through my mind, and my husband and I often discussed them. As we traveled to events and conferences all over the world, coming across like-minded individuals who had similar concerns was encouraging. Many of the same questions around the new international cultural exchange came up in conversations with others, so we decided to elevate these personal discussions to a larger forum. We would invite experts and discuss these baseline questions in a professional framework. My belief that cultural differences among people are best overcome through personal exchange is constantly being reaffirmed; only through conversations with others can we see and understand their point of view. That was one reason we created the German-Egyptian Cultural Forum in 2001 in Cairo. The forum ended up being a main point of reference for the many international cultural conferences that the Bertelsmann Foundation would subsequently launch.[23]

In the context of supporting a worldwide cultural exchange, I started a series of conferences with the Bertelsmann Foundation under the heading Corporate Cultures in Global Interaction. Over the years this series grew into a well-respected forum for addressing cultural and economic issues.[24] We were especially interested in hearing from Asian countries, whose newfound economic strength is changing the world's political landscape. As the global balance shifts, the U.S.-led West is no longer determining the rules of the game.

One of our first large forums, titled "The Impact of Globalization on Cultural Identity in Business," took place in April 2001 in Tokyo, in the context of supporting a German-Japanese dialogue.[25] In 2002 we held a workshop called "Global Business Culture" in Gütersloh,[26] and in Berlin in 2004 we organized "Experiences in Business." These workshops took a closer look at the effects of globalization on Germany and examined the challenges in store for those in leadership positions. The corporate culture that my husband put into place at Bertelsmann is especially relevant in the current climate of globalization. He overhauled the company's working environment by delegating more responsibilities to the employees, supporting a true partnership between employer and employee, and encouraging the workforce to identify with and invest in the company's goals.

In 2004 we held a German-Chinese conference in Beijing that focused on examining cultural differences. Its motto was "Learn from each other to work with each other." I was very impressed by China's enormous economic growth, its cultural traditions, and its extreme organization and efficiency, as well as the personal encounters I had with the conference participants. About 120 political, cultural, and economic leaders took part in the Beijing conference. It closed with a gala concert, held in conjunction with the Beijing music festival, featuring performances by the Chinese and European participants of Bertelsmann's New Voices contest.

At the conference, I was reunited with the former Chinese minister of culture Sun Jiazheng, whom I first met in 2002 and with whom I am still friendly. I again encountered his unmatched generosity and hospitality during the Olympic Games in 2008, when he spent more than two hours meeting with me—which is a long time in the busy schedule of the host of one of the world's largest events. I saw how personal interactions and a deep respect for the other's achievements can open doors in the complex relationship between China and Europe. When two countries with such different cultures engage in a dialogue, their different perspectives must be granted a clear voice. Only then can we truly understand each other's values and traditions; only then can we develop new strategies for working together. Openness, tolerance, and the willingness to learn are the prerequisites for avoiding misunderstandings and developing a mutual trust.[27]

India, another Asian economic powerhouse, was at the center of our International Cultural Forum in 2005 in New Delhi.[28] Here we discussed the specific circumstances for an Indian-European dialogue, and the convergence of Indian and European perspectives on the global challenges in the economic, political, and cultural realms. The forum grew out of the close collaboration among the Bertelsmann Foundation, the Rajiv Gandhi Foundation, and the Nand and Jeet Khemka Foundation. This cultural exchange project, too, ended with a concert by participants in our New Voices contest. Many new bridges between Europe and India were built during this forum, and the collaboration continues in numerous ongoing projects.

This forum was marked by remarkable encounters with leading personalities in science, culture, and politics. One meeting, especially, was unforgettable. I had an appointment to meet with Sonia Gandhi, but it was canceled at the last minute—she was unavailable. I was disappointed but continued with my order of the day. That afternoon I was talking with some conference participants on my hotel's terrace when the ambassador suddenly stood before me. Mrs. Gandhi was able to see me after all, but it would have to be the next day at five P.M. Twenty minutes were allotted. Of course I said yes.

The next day I was picked up at the prearranged time and was driven in a number of vehicles, which I had to change several times, to Mrs. Gandhi's residence. The building was quite remarkable for its modesty, which is unusual for an Indian manor house. I had to wait in several reception rooms before I could finally join Mrs. Gandhi in the library. She sat at a long table, her body framed by back lighting. I will always remember the moment she stood up. My Indian contacts had warned me that talking to Mrs. Gandhi could be arduous, and that the exchange could be dry. So I began telling her the story of the house of Bertelsmann. I told her about the work the company does, the development of the foundation, and our commitment to societal reforms. I also told her about my work. We spoke very openly about the people from whom we took advice and discussed the criteria we used to choose members of our boards. She told me that she takes advice only from scientists, and I advised her to speak with businessmen or -women as well. "But they cannot be corrupt," she countered. It was not easy to choose the right collaborators in India.

For a long time we spoke about how we judged people; it was a very open and moving conversation. When we finished, an hour and a half had passed. We stood under an oil painting of the founder of independent India, Nehru, and she spoke to me about the fates of political dynasties. She also told me about her son, who was active in India's parliament. I was admiring a small sculpture of a mother and child that stood beneath the painting of Nehru, when Sonia Gandhi picked the sculpture up and placed it in my hand. "I want to give this to you," she suddenly said. "I cannot accept that," I replied. "Yes, you can. I will find something else for this spot."

It was a very moving moment. Today the small sculpture stands in my office underneath a portrait of my husband. Whenever I look at it, I vividly remember that afternoon in India. To me, that day represents what a human encounter can accomplish. When two friends interact, some bias may still color their perception, but then they may discover something that connects them, and they realize that they have similar thoughts and questions. As a connection is made, their exchange becomes light and effortless. These kinds of encounters give us hope that not all is lost in this world of competing interests.

Over the decades, I came to also greatly value Mikhail

Gorbachev, the president of the former Soviet Union. My husband and I met Mr. and Mrs. Gorbachev in the spring of 1992, on the occasion of the publication of his book at Bertelsmann.[29] Our first meeting was warm and sincere. I was very much moved by Gorbachev's passionate commitment to the democratization of Russia, the fall of the Wall, and the subsequent reunification of Europe. He, too, had a strong woman at his side: his wife, the philosophy professor Raisa Gorbachev, whom I admired greatly, and whose untimely death in 1999 filled my husband and me with great sorrow.

In addition to our initiatives in Asia and the Middle East, we took a great number of trips to, and met with business partners and political allies in, Europe. Bertelsmann has especially close ties to Spain, which go back almost fifty years. After some initial contacts, my husband founded the book club Círculo de Lectores in 1962 in Barcelona. To this day, it is one of the largest and oldest book clubs in the Spanish-speaking world. It was also Bertelsmann's first business establishment in a non-German-speaking region. The Círculo de Lectores marked the beginning of our international activities. But the book club was established not just as a financial investment. The educational assistance that came along with it proved to be very important to Spain's cultural development. Círculo de Lectores is still considered one of Bertelsmann's most effective pilot projects.[30]

Spain has always had a special place in our hearts; for many decades we vacationed on Majorca. In 1990, just as he did in his hometown of Gütersloh, my husband founded a city library in Majorca: the Biblioteca Can Torró. Within a few years the library had become a cultural magnet not only for residents but also for librarians, education officials, and experts from all over Spain. This overwhelmingly positive experience encouraged us in 1995 to create our own Spanish foundation, called Fundación Bertelsmann. Based in Barcelona, it promotes the countrywide modernization of libraries, educational exchanges between schools and libraries, and literacy.[31]

Above and beyond library science, the Fundación Bertelsmann went on to create numerous social projects that help support the profound changes that globalization has brought. Spain's crown family have repeatedly commended our work with special recognition, and we now have a decades-long history of an intensive and enriching exchange to look back on.[32]

News of Bertelsmann's work in Spain spread to South America, and here, too, we were fortunate enough to have some fascinating and illuminating encounters. We made a special friend in Roberto Costa de Abreu Sodré, the former governor of São Paulo who later was the foreign minister of Brazil, and whose warmth, generosity, and tremendous hospitality I will never forget.

One can never truly get to know a country's culture

through official visits alone. Personal encounters, people's habits and gestures, tell us more about a country than any book ever could. During these encounters, a tradition shows itself, past and present merge to create unforgettable moments, and a country's culture can fully come alive.

My husband and I also developed a special connection with the United States over the course of many decades. As a young prisoner of war in the American POW camp Concordia in Kansas, my husband learned the true meaning of democracy and of civilian democratic engagement.[33] This experience influenced his life and his business decisions and played a large role in his commitment to the foundation. The basic tenets of our humanity and our intrinsic freedom come from mutual respect and from taking a view to both the past and the future. The Bertelsmann Foundation's objective of creating international channels of communication was a way to bring about not only the reconciliation with Israel but a transatlantic partnership with the United States.

During our many transatlantic trips over twenty years, we established and developed numerous initiatives. A highlight was the opening of a branch of the Bertelsmann Foundation in Washington, D.C., in 2008.[34] The Bertelsmann Foundation North America—an independent foundation according to U.S. law—seeks to support the international debate around the risks and opportunities of globalization with specific projects and conferences. It also aims to extend the long tradition of the German-American friendship far into the future. A very special friend and companion in this endeavor was Henry Kissinger.[35] Every exchange of ideas with him is incredibly inspiring; his vast experience and his deep understanding of human nature turn every conversation into a truly special occasion. I also very much enjoyed working with Kofi Annan. A master of diplomacy, all of Kofi's endeavors are marked by his passion for bringing people together and for finding even the smallest common denominator in the most desperate situations. As a mediator among different religions and cultures, he has always been my guide.

The growth of globalization challenges all of us. The conflicts among different cultures and the contest over global distribution may lead the world toward violence and chaos; but perhaps we can secure peaceful cooperation among the many different cultures. It is especially important to me to encourage exchange between Europe and the United States to support our next generation of leaders. Each new generation must prove again and again that it is able to take part in a dialogue. The bridges that were built by the postwar generation on both sides of the Atlantic must remain stable long into the future; there will never be a substitute for democracy and for commitment to humanity.[36]

Medical and Health Care Projects

Not in the least because of what I went through with my own family, I developed a great interest in medical issues. When our youngest son, Andreas, was seven years old, he was diagnosed during a routine medical checkup with uveitis, an inflammation of the middle layer of the eye. The disease progresses in surges and can cause chronic vision impairment. In the worst cases, it can lead to the detachment of the retina and result in blindness. At the time, uveitis was considered incurable. During the disease's acute phase, our son endured torturous headaches and extremely painful eyestrain; he could not see and of course couldn't play or horse around. For weeks at a time, he wasn't allowed to go to school.

As a mother, it broke my heart to see Andreas suffer so, and our family lived in fear of him losing his sight. We were in constant contact with specialists, but his doctor, Professor Boeke from the eye clinic in Kiel, gave us little hope. He and his colleagues did not know of any cure.

In those days, cortisone was used to lessen the impact of the illness, though it did not combat it directly. Our search for alternative medicines proved futile as well. I was desperate. Was our son going to go blind?

In 1980 we took a family vacation on the Seychelles Islands. Here we noticed that another ailment that Andreas had, a pronounced case of eczema, got visibly better even without cortisone treatment. Within a few days, the affected areas were completely healed. Back in Germany, Andreas's attending eye doctor noticed great improvement in his eyes as well, and my son was able to regain his full focal strength.

What had happened? The climate specific to the Seychelles, the warmth, the intense light, the sea air—something must have had a great impact on our son's condition. When I spoke with Andreas's doctors, I became charged. Suddenly there was hope that others affected with this illness could be helped as well, with climate or light therapy. This prospect inspired me enormously. At the time, approximately 200,000 people in the Federal Republic of Germany suffered from uveitis; the cost of treatment was in the millions. In 1981, following my initiative, the Bertelsmann Foundation established the Uveitis Project.[37] Under its auspices, in 1981, 1985, and 1986 two groups of uveitis patients traveled under medical supervision to the Dead Sea in Israel. The pilot project demonstrated that exposure to the particular light of the region led to a decrease in symptoms and at times even to a cure.

In 1984, we founded the German Uveitis Study Group in Gütersloh, which was made up mostly of ophthalmologists from different university hospitals. The group's goal was to expand research, information, and education around the diagnosis and treatment of uveitis. We formed the first uveitis self-help group in Germany in the summer of 1986 in Gütersloh. At the time this was a new type of program, and the group has since served as an example for many other self-help groups. Almost exactly four years later I became president of the German Uveitis Association, founded in July 1990. In the years that followed, the association started a number of research projects that promoted the development of outpatient light therapy, including one at the University of Münster. The uveitis project was the first health care initiative of the Bertelsmann Foundation.[38]

This first success, which grew directly out of my personal observations and my intuitive sense, encouraged me to continue along this somewhat unconventional way of gathering expert knowledge. The uveitis project taught me to draw on international specialists and to seek out unusual partners—whatever it took to support a project.

The whole time that I was working on the uveitis project, I was also very involved in the field of neurological illness.[39] Once again, I was motivated by personal experience. When one of my sons was fourteen years old, he began to show signs of motor skill difficulties. Eventually the left side of his body became paralyzed. We were frozen with fear. Would our son become an invalid? Six weeks later he could walk again, but no neurologist had an explanation for what had happened.

At this time I knew very little about seizures and strokes, and the disease was not part of public knowledge. Fortunately this was not our son's diagnosis. Instead, his doctors suspected that he had contracted Lyme disease from a tick bite. But when the neurologists I met during my son's illness asked for my support for a project to determine the early detection of a stroke or seizure, the powerlessness we felt then made me eager to help.

In August 1983 I met with the neurologist and psychiatrist Prof. Dr. Gerhard Sitzer and with the foundation's executive director, Dr. Hans-Dieter Weger, to discuss the possibility of the Bertelsmann Foundation's involvement in the field of neurology.[40] In 1984 we supported a project by the Düsseldorf University Hospital; we funded a number of studies that analyzed the blood flow in the carotid artery. These studies would assist in properly assessing arteriosclerotic vascular disease and determine an individual's risk for a stroke. The project, titled Neurology I, ran from 1984 until 1987. For a project called Neurology II, from 1985 until 1988, the Bertelsmann Foundation supported research at the Clinic for Neurology at the University of Münster, this time to discover the warning signs of an imminent stroke. The foundation granted financial assistance and supported the acquisition of the necessary technology. For a third foundation project, called Neurology III, the university clinics of Mannheim and Münster used blood samples to determine the causes of thrombosis, or a blood clot, which can trigger a stroke.

Looking back, the research projects may seem fairly straightforward. But at the time, I was not only very involved but emotionally invested. In the beginning, I was constantly seeking out leading health professionals to gather information on vascular disease and strokes. I wanted to know everything! Slowly I learned more and more about this treacherous and widespread illness, which is the third leading cause of death in Germany. According to official statistics of that time, each year 250,000 to 300,000 people suffered from a stroke. Every fifth person died, and only a quarter of those affected were ever able to go back to work. The real number must actually be much higher, since not every stroke is diagnosed as such.

The more time I spent dealing with cardiovascular disease, the more I realized how many taboos existed around it. Whenever I spoke to someone about it, they often became quite uncomfortable. Everyone thought it affected only older people. Indeed, it is a frightening thought to perhaps one day have a crooked smile, struggle to speak, or even be paralyzed. But it didn't happen very often, did it? And anyway, it was a problem for old people, not a current medical phenomenon for younger people, right?

Actually, the opposite is true. When I began to visit hospitals and rehabilitation centers where stroke victims were being treated, I realized the extent of the challenges. Both the population and the doctors knew way too little about stroke's cause. It's not only older persons who are afflicted (and their number is growing); young people, children, even a fetus in the womb can have a stroke. In my engagement with the cause, I encountered desperate patients and families. They are unforgettable. Working for stroke victims had by then long been my passion, and I realized that apoplexy, or stroke, needed its own lobby. I spoke at length with my husband about it. While he understood the urgency of the situation, he let me know in no uncertain terms that any research program into the causes of an illness, coupled with an effective public campaign and outreach program, would put a long-term strain on the resources of the Bertelsmann Foundation. I had to take on the responsibility of expanding the initiative to other funding sources.

I thought long and hard about the best way to set up a trust for this type of endeavor. Would I really be able to generate public awareness for such a challenging issue? Finally, on November 17, 1992, the independent German

Stroke Aid Foundation was established. On January 29, 1993, it was accredited by the minister of the interior of North Rhine–Westphalia.[41]

Now, after seventeen years of working with the Stroke Aid Foundation, I know that our long journey was worth it. The beginning was hard—I often had to get up between four and five in the morning to keep my many appointments with doctors, sponsors, and project partners. Without a doubt, the name *Mohn* and my connection to the house of Bertelsmann helped open doors. But it was up to the Stroke Aid Foundation to seal the deal.[42]

Over the years, I was able to get some important representatives of the German economy on board with us. To this day, our backers include chairmen and chairwomen of major corporations and small-business leaders, as well as compassionate individuals. All of our patrons have dedicated themselves to our cause, and only with their tireless support were we able to rigorously expand the Stroke Aid Foundation. In addition, volunteers from all over the country dedicate their time and their pro-social engagement to pursue our objective and bring our cause to the public. Together with representatives from the fields of politics, health care, medicine, science, and culture we were able to generate enormous public awareness of the disease. This awareness is vital for fighting the causes of stroke and for improving prevention, acute care, and victim rehabilitation.

The foundation works both nationally and internationally to coordinate activities around stroke research and treatment. It also acts as a network, and is especially supportive of model projects. Furthermore, the foundation supports many measures that improve the quality of care for stroke victims, such as the nationwide creation of stroke centers and the establishment of a comprehensive treatment protocol.

We have accomplished a great deal, but there is still a lot left to do. Even though we have contributed greatly to the prevention and treatment of strokes, the continued aging of our society means that the number of yearly stroke victims remains unchanged, at 200,000. Every three minutes someone has a stroke, and every nine minutes someone dies from one. It is still the third most common cause of death. In the face of the increased graying of our society, these are alarming numbers. By the year 2030, it is estimated that there will be twice as many instances of stroke among those sixty-five and older, and the German health system will face enormous challenges. The Bertelsmann Foundation is continuously engaged in a discourse with hospitals and insurance companies, and we continue to study how the fragmentation of our health care system leads to missed opportunities.

The German Stroke Aid Foundation tirelessly works toward finding sustainable solutions for stroke aid. Our social mandate calls for developing and supporting all medical services, so that quick and professional help can be provided to everyone. Beyond that, we are committed to supporting disease prevention and to funding innovative diagnoses and therapies.

Just as it was seventeen years ago, continuous professional development around stroke research is essential for saving lives. Any gap in medical knowledge can pose a danger for a stroke victim, for every minute counts when dealing with a stroke. Thus the establishment of nationwide specialized stroke centers is one of our most urgent goals. These so-called stroke units can establish an integrated treatment plan in the disease's early stages. A treatment plan includes a quick and assured diagnosis, followed by multidisciplinary treatment. We are very proud that the stroke units that we initiated have improved patients' prognoses by 25 percent.

One of the foundation's main responsibilities will always be to create public awareness and to do fund-raising, which includes finding new donors and maintaining ties to old ones. To create public awareness, we work closely with the print media, television, radio, and Internet. Our carefully chosen charity events, like the Bertelsmann AG Rose Ball, the Semper Opera Ball (which chose us as a charity partner in 2008), and the golf charity tournament called Ein Schlag gegen den Schlag (A Stroke Against the Stroke), raise a generous amount of funds to support and advance our work.

My personal commitment to this cause has proven to be a full-time job. Endless travel, along with thousands of phone calls and meetings, are all part of my work. But I get back a thousandfold of what I put in. And as happy as I am with all that we've accomplished, I do know that this disease will keep us very busy in the years to come. I am pleased and grateful to everyone who continues to support our efforts.

My involvement with Stroke Aid made me very aware of the issue of preventive health care. It was very important to me that Bertelsmann lead by example, so we were the first company to offer its employees a stroke checkup. About seventeen hundred of our workers took advantage of it and had an examination. The results were alarming. Twenty-five percent of those examined were overweight and/or had high blood pressure and thus belonged to a risk group that had to be put under a doctor's care.

Between 1996 and 1997, the German Stroke Aid Foundation, together with a number of corporate health care plans, organized a pilot study that took place at several large German corporations. We asked the insured employees to undergo a free preventive care health exam, and more than five thousand of them did.[43] The study demonstrated that it is indeed possible to recruit large numbers of people to take preventive measures. In the face of escalating health care costs, preventive care is paramount for reducing costs. Based on my experiences with the German Stroke Aid Foundation (which is now led by my daughter, Brigitte, as its chairwoman), I was able to launch a number of projects and initiatives within the Bertelsmann Foundation. Following my husband's wish, in June 1989 I launched a project in support of chiropractic medicine. Working closely with the University of Münster, in October 1994 we were finally able to open an academy for the advancement of chiropractic medicine, which provides training, research, and education.[44]

Soon afterward I initiated another health care project based on my personal observations. In the late 1980s, little was known about the effects of minerals and trace elements on the body.[45] I learned about it when my husband became ill. I assembled experts from all over Europe, which led to the Bertelsmann Foundation's project Minerals and Trace Elements. Running from 1990 to 2000, the initiative created tremendous public awareness. Today the effects of trace elements and minerals are common knowledge.

To this day, the research and promotion of healthy lifestyles is a main focus of the Bertelsmann Foundation's health care topic area. My daughter, Brigitte, now leads this area, with great expertise and enthusiasm.[46] So much still needs be done in preschools, schools, workplaces, and communities to increase health awareness from an early age and to integrate healthy behavior into people's daily lives. The Bertelsmann Foundation has launched a number of programs to start a dialogue with political leaders and to promote local and national health initiatives. But our work is still cut out for us. Despite numerous efforts, healthy lifestyle choices are still not adequately promoted in schools. Many students have to deal with health issues like overweight or gross motor skill deficiency.

In addition, when compared to students internationally, German students are still not achieving their stated educational goals. Teachers complain of increased stress levels in the classroom, and many are suffering from burn-out as early as their fifties. For these and other reasons, the Bertelsmann Foundation is seeking major reforms in the area of student health. We initiated Anschub.de as a regionally led but nationally applicable alliance of institutes in health and education. It is our common goal to create new incentives to foster the improvement of health care concerns in German schools.

After two years of project preparation, we have now begun to implement some practical solutions at several schools in pilot regions. A close collaboration among students, parents, teachers, and the administration is a must in order for the project to be successful. We hope that this pilot project will create new incentives for providing continuing education and training for teachers and school administrators, and that we can continue to advance these directives across the country.

In the corporate culture that my husband developed at Bertelsmann, a main objective is to promote the idea that the partnership between employer and employee includes a company's health care policy. In these times of global economic challenges, many employees face increased responsibility, greater self-reliance, and more critical input at their place of employment. At first glance, this may sound ideal, especially when doing meaningful work. But realistically, for many workers this new independence leads to an expedited work pace, an increase in stress, and mounting insecurity. In light of this growing discrepancy between an individual's wish for meaningful employment and the reality of today's quickly changing workplace conditions, the Bertelsmann Foundation founded a commission of experts to investigate the future of corporate health care policy. Beyond general health care issues, the commission worked to identify the economic, social, and personal challenges that lie ahead for workers. Together with the Hans-Böckler-Stiftung, the commission launched a research group called the Initiative for Company Health Care Policy. It went on to develop a ten-point program to reform mandatory automobile insurance.

Our next project, called Contemporary Company

Health Care Policy, grew from ecommendations by the commission. Instituting medical exams for executives is as much a part of our project as the funding and implementation of preventive health care programs within companies. Special notice must also be given to our project A Healthy Workplace During Demographic Change, which we created together with the Hans-Böckler-Stiftung and the New Quality of Work Initiative (INQA). With this project, we established a number of regional support facilities to maintain the health and productivity of the aging workforce over the long term. At these sites, small and midsize businesses have easy access to information about company health care policies.

The issue of nationwide improvement of corporate health care is to this day very dear to me. I have often wondered how to best implement the many different standards that corporations have for health care and preventive care in the face of today's global challenges. For these policies in turn reflect attitudes toward issues of work-life balance—and the different ways these issues are handled are immense.

This is why in 2001 I created an international business network called Enterprise for Health.[47] I was delighted to see this enterprise grow into the only business network of its kind in Europe. The group's task was to examine workers' health, motivation, and productivity in the context of economic and psychosocial factors. The ongoing global economic crisis has intensified many workers' anxieties. Recent surveys have shown that young people, especially, view their working conditions as extremely demanding. In fact, many do not believe they will retire in good health. Especially alarming is that people fear losing their job more than they fear risking their health.[48] This is a shocking indication of how much our values have changed, not only in our society but in the whole working world. The importance of our Enterprise for Health initiative can therefore not be underestimated. An international survey of the employees of Bertelsmann AG confirmed the close relationship among a partnership-based corporate structure and employee motivation and creativity, achievement, flexibility, and mental and physical well-being. Factors like the delegation of responsibility, creative freedom, and the opportunity for creative input contributed greatly to employee satisfaction and engagement. A well-run business not only does well financially; its employees are also less often sick![49]

Personal incentive leads to financial success and vice versa. Having both can have a significant positive impact on an employee's health. As we look toward the future, we as a society need innovative and strong businesses that are financially sound and can plan fiscally for the long term. The Enterprise for Health initiative contributed greatly to this understanding, as it demonstrated that workplace quality is an integral part of modern corporate structure.

My greatest hope is that employers and employees will find a new rapport, one that is rooted in personal responsibility and self-determination as well as solidarity and compassion. We will have made great strides if we not only generate new directions for health care management but stay the course in these difficult economic times. Any business that establishes its health care policies within the paradigm of a partnership-based corporate culture leads the way to a forward-looking, compassionate society.

Music and Cultural Projects

Since childhood I have been fascinated by the strength and beauty of the human voice. When I was little, I was thrilled whenever my mother sang with us. As a young girl, I greatly enjoyed singing with my friends, and now that I am older, everything from pop music to classic arias can put a spell on me. I was grateful to be able to share my passion for music with my husband, who himself had a lovely singing voice.

Again and again I saw, on the many international trips I took, how much music is able to connect people across national, ethnic, and linguistic divides. I find great solace and strength in music, which has always helped me through my darkest hours.

In 1985 we held a ceremony to celebrate the 150-year anniversary of the Bertelsmann publishing house, and we invited Herbert von Karajan and the Berlin Philharmonic to give a concert at the Gütersloh town hall. During a talk after the concert, the maestro lamented how difficult it is to find young operatic talent. While many fields promote the search for new talent, there is still a great need for new young voices for opera. The thought of helping out in this area electrified me. It seemed like a perfect project for the Bertelsmann Foundation.

When I discussed this idea with my husband, he was just as excited as I was. But after the initial euphoria subsided, I began to realize that the plan would likely turn into an enormous and time-consuming undertaking. Undoubtedly I would need to create professional partnerships and connect with well-known institutions in the opera world to turn this plan into reality. My most important partner was August Everding, the general intendant of the Bavarian state theaters. From our first phone conversation, he was 100 percent with me. From his decades-long experience as an opera director, he was very familiar with the problem of the lack of future talent. As the president of the German Theater Union and of the Bavarian Theater Academy, his opinion carried great weight. Having August Everding on your side meant having the support of a courageous and tireless ally.

During a meeting in Munich, August Everding explained to me that worldwide there is no single competition for young singers that offered orchestral accompaniment. Such accompaniment is essential to young, classically trained singers so that they may assess their stage presence—indispensable to a professional career as an opera singer. But most auditions still took place in the small dusty rooms of a music academy, which were unlocked just for this occasion. They usually took place with only piano accompaniment—the young singers couldn't even dream of having a full orchestra accompany them. A true contest under live-performance conditions was needed, where up-and-coming singers could test their presence on a large stage.

During my lively discussions with August Everding, the idea of the Bertelsmann Foundation's New Voices international singing competition was born. Working closely with the German Theater Union, August Everding began assembling a talent pool of national and international young opera singers. A jury of opera professionals was formed, made up of directors, music critics, and artists who are still well known today. The jury included Elisabeth Legge-Schwarzkopf, Hans Pischner, James Wagner, Josef Metternich, Brigitte Fassbaender, Erika Köth, Edda Moser, Birgit Nilsson, Thomas M. Stein, Hellmuth Matiasek, Francisco Araiza, Sir George Christie, René Kollo, Gérard Mortier, Hans Hirsch, Christoph Groszer, Nicholas Payne, Siegfried Jerusalem, Dominique Meyer, Evamaria Wieser, Bernd Loebe, Jürgen Kesting, and Anja Silja. August Everding was jury president until his death in 1999.

From the beginning, our intent was to support young talent by televising broadcasts of their performances and by inviting talent agents and artistic directors to the competitions. Our first Europe-wide New Voices competition took place in 1987 in Gütersloh.[50] The contest was open to anyone who studied voice at a European music conservatory. After several rounds of preselection, thirty-six participants from the Federal Republic of Germany, Austria, Switzerland, France, Italy, England, Poland, Bulgaria, Sweden, Canada, the United States, and Japan took part in the final contest.

What began as a European event grew into a worldwide undertaking in the 1990s. Since then, the preselections have taken place in various cities around the world. Whether in Tokyo or in Washington, in Sydney or in St. Petersburg, the New Voices contest grew so quickly that in 2001, for the first time, singers from five continents took part in the competition. It turns out that our singing contest, too, experienced the effects of globalization. Especially the East Bloc countries have come up with a tremendous number of extremely talented young singers. Since 1995, we have been working closely with the Yokosuka Art Theater Foundation in Japan. One hundred and fifty contestants from Korea, Taiwan, Japan, and Indonesia participate in the preselection competition. And since 1997, the Chinese elimination rounds have been impeccably organized and fully supported by China's cultural ministry.[51]

For all the participants, the road to the biannual competition in Gütersloh is long and labor intensive. They must learn three arias from an opera or an operetta both for the semifinals and for the final round. In 2009, on two successive concert evenings, forty-one selected singers each sang two arias before a jury.

Our New Voices competition quickly established itself as one of the most sought-after musical events among both the general public and classical music experts. We invite about nine hundred guests from politics, finance, culture, and media to join the festivities. From the beginning, our guests have included artistic directors of major opera companies, international talent agents, and representatives of the press, television, and radio. The final performances take place in a concert hall, but so do the recitals with piano: no longer are they tucked away in the small room of a music academy. They are heard through the entire week of competition on the main stage. Since 1995 Gustav Kuhn, director of the Accademia di Montegral and the Erl Tyrolean Festival, has been the competition's artistic director.

Starting in 1999, Brian Dickie, the general director of the Chicago Opera Theater, has been a regular member of our jury. For many years, he also led the international preselection. Brian cuts a path through mediocrity. Finding new voices is his passion, and he ceaselessly circles the globe to follow his calling. For them, a promising new talent must possess more than just an excellent voice. He looks at a singer's demeanor as a whole to see whether the performer is able to fully embody the music he or she is singing.

The things we experienced in those years! Sudden illnesses, problems with visas, lost suitcases, and forgotten sheet music kept me and my team on our toes. We spent endless time sharing the fear and apprehension of our young singers, and just as many hours engaged in lively discussions about the finalists. For me personally, the town hall of Gütersloh has been a magical place for the last twenty-two years. My other duties can wait. Memories often come flooding back to me, like that of Nathalie Stutzmann, the winner of our first competition in 1987. She is now considered the most important contralto singer, is invited to perform all over the world, and has won numerous international prizes, including the Grammy Award. We discovered Vesselina Kasarova, who won the competition in 1989 and is now one of the world's most in-demand mezzo-sopranos. And the winner in 1995, Gwyn Hughes Jones, has since given a brilliant performance at the Salzburg Festival and has performed on European as well as American stages. In 2007 we were enchanted by the young Latvian singer Marina Rebeka, who is now fully booked until the year 2015.

These young singers' complete dedication to fulfilling their life's dream has always moved me. During the pre-selection rounds as well as the final round of judging, equal weight is placed on technical know-how, musical presentation, voice quality, artistic personality, and stage presence. Especially for contests with many international participants, it was very important to me that once the competition was over, we didn't lose sight of the newly discovered young talent. New singers can easily get caught up in competing for the best roles in the opera world, then ruin their most valuable asset—their voice. So in 1997 we established an international master class that takes place in the year between the biannual competitions. In the class, up to fifteen former participants of the New Voices contest can train their voices under the guidance of world-renowned musicians without any competitive pressure. In the class they can carefully hone their voices and their vocal expression, as well as work on their interpretation and stage presence.

In addition to musical study, the young singers receive expert advice about topics such as securing an agent, auditioning, and contractual and tax law. A singer must be well equipped on many levels in order to stay successful in the international world of opera. The Bertelsmann Foundation is very committed to preparing young opera talent on all levels. Whenever I see one of our young singing stars perform years later on one of the world's great opera stages, it makes me very happy.

Without a doubt, New Voices has been a success story. Since the beginning, our goal has been to meet and exceed the highest artistic standards. We have committed ourselves to transparency and to being fair to all contestants. We view our competition as a tool for cross-cultural communication, and we maintain complete tolerance for cultural diversity and the rights of the individual.

We have come a long way, and today New Voices is recognized all over the world.[52] I always think with love and gratitude of my husband, Reinhard Mohn. Without his deep belief in the unifying power of music, his tireless support of the creative contest, his vision, and his courage, this idea would not have come to fruition.

The Liz Mohn Foundation
for Culture and Music

A survey undertaken by the Bertelsmann Foundation found that two-thirds of Germany's population considers the funding of classical music and opera an important part of our society.[53] While it is still mostly older or well-educated persons who are especially passionate about classical music and opera, 67 percent of the population nevertheless takes notice of classical music when it is played on the radio or on television. Classical music, the survey found, is generally considered to have an important cultural value. We generally consider the backers to be foundations, private sponsors, and patrons of the arts. The support of musical faculties in children is considered particularly significant. Indeed, 64 percent of those surveyed found it crucial to expose children from as early as kindergarten to the art of professional singing. The funding of live performances at popular locations was considered highly relevant as well. This survey spoke to my heart and encouraged me to continue my work.

By 1997, I had initiated a pilot project for music education in schools and kindergartens.[54] At the time, this topic wasn't discussed much, but I noticed a glaring lack of musical education for children and young people. Everyone has been at a family gathering, with friends, or at a get-together, and when it's time to sing a song, only the older generation knows the words. The younger generation usually just stand there, feeling embarrassed. Young people today often do not possess even the most basic musical knowledge, which used to be passed on from generation to generation through communal singing.

Together with the Ministry of Education of North Rhine–Westphalia, we developed and tested a number of innovative yet practical teaching methods, along with classroom materials. In the course of developing these methods, we realized how important musical proficiency is for children's overall development of cognitive and social skills. This knowledge encouraged me greatly. When the project ended in 2004, I knew I had to continue the work. I began to think about a new foundation of my own.

In November 2005, the time had come. The Liz Mohn Foundation for Culture and Music[55] was ready to begin its work. I wanted to continue what we accomplished with the New Voices contest, but with a focus on the contest's culturally integrative and pedagogical qualities.

Thus, the foundation mostly supports musical education and funds projects to support the musical development of children and youth. I firmly believe that music has the power to make everyone equal, to overcome our differences in heritage, education, and class.

Two of the biggest challenges in our society are the integration of immigrants into a community and mutual understanding between people of different cultural backgrounds. The Liz Mohn Foundation for Culture and Music is continually on the lookout for project ideas to encourage institutions, associations, alliances, foundations, and individual initiatives and their leaders to take appropriate actions that rise to these challenges. One of our main criteria for launching a new program is that the children and young people who are involved actively participate in the execution of every phase, and that the project be an example of true cultural integration.

Much remains to be done in regional culture development and young talent recruitment. The Boys Choir of Gütersloh, founded in 2007, is especially close to my heart. Today more than sixty boys between the ages of six and thirteen sing in the choir. Depending on the boys' age, choir practice is held once or twice a week, and the children also receive individual or small-group lessons. Choir weekends and retreats not only delve deeper into musical study but also nurture groups. Our first trips to

European foreign countries, along with a number of public concerts and even some television performances, have shown us that we are on the right track.

Many successful artists begin their careers early in life, but providing artists with a musical education is not enough. To protect and nurture their potential, we must stay by their side and grant them ongoing artistic support. My experience with the New Voices competition taught me how important this type of support is, in order not to lose our prized young artists as they enter the grueling contest for the biggest roles. Many young singers don't give their voices enough time to mature; they take on parts that are too demanding and after just a few years are left with their instrument ruined.

I wanted to keep this from happening, so since 2007 the Liz Mohn Foundation for Culture and Music has been a backer of the International Opera Studio at the Staatsoper Unter den Linden. Under the artistic direction of Daniel Barenboim, the Opera Studio offers promising young singers the opportunity to prepare themselves for a career in opera and musical theater.

The central objective of our sponsorship of young vocal talent is to support a young person's artistic and personal development. At the Opera Studio, students take on small and medium-size roles in productions at the Staatsoper and study specific opera parts. Their curriculum includes song workshops, individual classes with renowned singers and composers, and classes in dialogue and recital study, body and movement training, acting, and scene study. The students receive continuous feedback on their development. The Opera Studio gives young singers the opportunity to work as part of a company in a safe space, where they can test and develop their musical and artistic personalities.

The establishment of my culture and music foundation was the fulfillment of a personal dream of mine. In his autobiography, Daniel Barenboim wrote that music helps us discover something "about ourselves, about our society, about politics—in short, about the human being."[56] I can only agree wholeheartedly with this sentiment.

A Question of Belief: Religion and Spiritual Orientation in a Globalized World

My childhood was heavily informed by the Catholic faith. Every morning before school, my sister and I had to attend the seven o'clock service at our church. I spent many mornings very cold and rubbing the sleep from my eyes. At Christmastime, we had to be in church at five A.M.

These daily services were definitely not my cup of tea, and neither was our household's daily mealtime prayer, where all the children took turns saying grace. When it was my turn, I kept things short: "For this food and drink I give thanks. Amen." These identical, repetitive rituals bored me. However, I was fascinated by the Catholic Church's religious festivals, with their lush pageantry and their tremendous spirit of community. These traditions gave me a feeling of security and great joy. Whenever I was lucky enough to be a flower girl for the Eucharist procession, it meant spring had begun. Around Christmas, I experienced feelings of joyful expectation along with peaceful, familiar comfort. This warmth had nothing to do with presents. During wartime, sometimes the only thing on the gift table was a head of cabbage—we had nothing else. But my mother didn't need much to fill our house with love. Even in our darkest hours, she sang Christmas carols with us and told us about the meaning of Christmas.

Without doubt, a faith-based community and a connection to tradition can give us a valuable moral framework. This is how we learn the meaning of humanity and being part of a society. These communal rituals are part of our living history. They are cultural treasures that have been passed down over hundreds of years from generation to generation; they give us our social and personal identities. But the cataclysms of the twentieth century, two devastating world wars and their consequences, have permanently unsettled the image of Christian man throughout Europe.

The older I became, the more my own doubts grew. I often felt abandoned by my youthful Catholic beliefs, for they could not provide answers to the challenges I faced in my young adult life. When my daughter, Brigitte, was so severely ill with asthma that it almost cost her life, I was desperate. Like millions of other people in such straits, I asked myself: Why does God allow such suffering? The ancient question of Job is a despair over God's will that overcomes us in our most difficult times. There is no easy answer to this question; it is one that every person must answer for themselves, using their faith and conviction.

I am critical of some of the things that the Catholic Church stands for today. The current debates around its failings demonstrate that the church could benefit from some development and renewal. But for all the criticism aimed at the institution of the church, it has become more and more apparent to me over the years that a society cannot exist without spiritual guidance and a life-affirming foundation of moral values. Every religion in the world conveys this type of moral code, each in its own way.

My first trip to Israel made me acutely aware of how much my Catholic upbringing narrowed my horizons. Jerusalem is the only city in the world that is the birthplace of three world religions. What would have become of me had I been born here? Nobody can choose where they were born and raised. We are cast into our world and must live with its religious, political, and social order. Shouldn't this fact alone be our impetus for absolute religious tolerance?

Jerusalem's former mayor Teddy Kollek was tireless in his efforts to help the people of his city attain greater social stability, cultural acceptance, and personal pride, no matter what their religion. I saw in him an important role model. My later travels through Asia also deeply impressed me and gave me much to think about. My husband and I had numerous conversations about our experiences and encounters in Jewish, Muslim, Buddhist, and Hindu communities.[57]

Due to the globalization of the last decades, different cultures and religions are interacting with one another more frequently than ever. People from the most diverse backgrounds, from different classes, and with various religious orientations live and work together. More than ever the questions remain: What values are intrinsic to our future intertwined lives? What gives our lives meaning? What values can help us deal with conflicts? All around the world, politicians, scientists, writers, and business-people are discussing the possibility of communicating across national, ethnic, cultural, and religious divides. I am convinced that such international communication is possible only when it fully respects the historic, cultural, and religious roots of a society.

In my experience, religious beliefs and customs play an especially large role in the formation of people's values. This led me to ask myself whether a society's religion wasn't the key to understanding its values, as well as its concept of God and other aspects of its way of life. Wouldn't examining a society's religion lay bare its elemental building blocks, ones that all cultures share, making them understandable to everyone? And doesn't this type of view into a culture offer up the chance to understand what connects people all over the world and what they have in common?

My husband and I had many lively discussions about these possibilities. Over the decades, in his books and in his articles, he consistently criticized people in politics and finance for their failure to communicate, and he insisted on a radical rethinking to prepare our society for the future. We agreed that a closer look at the religious lifeways among the world's many faiths could offer a greater understanding of today's global society. Beyond addressing the immediate issue of creating an understanding among different nations and people, my husband felt that combining democracy with a religious orientation could create a system powerful enough to stand up to threats from the world's authoritarian governments.

I agree with him wholeheartedly, for I am convinced that in the future a democracy has a chance only if it wins the hearts of its people—if its main priority is to take into account its citizens' needs. The current climate of political apathy in our country, however, and in much of Europe is testimony to how difficult it is to achieve this goal.

How can we resolve this dilemma? How do we find out what people's greatest needs are? In 2007 a survey done by the Bertelsmann Foundation gave us a first overview of the current state of religious beliefs in different countries. The survey was developed with an interdisciplinary tool that I initiated, the Religion Monitor.[58] With the help of experts from sociology, psychology, theology, and religion, we compared the level of a country's religious belief with the impact this belief had on people's daily life. What does religion mean to an individual? To what extent do people practice their personal religious beliefs? What impact does religion have on society? These and other questions were answered by the Religion Monitor of the Bertelsmann Foundation.

The study interviewed over 21,000 people in twenty-one countries. Actual persons talked very specifically about their lives and their worldviews and what gave their personal lives meaning. They stood in for millions of people around the globe. The Religion Monitor gives us great insight into the religions of the world and enables us to be a part of its many different cultures.

In 2009 the Bertelsmann Foundation published the results of the Religion Monitor survey, with commentary, as *What Does the World Believe In?*[59] The results had surprised us. The cultures and religions that we surveyed offered up many similar concepts of religious belief, most of which were structured around the commitment to leading a responsible life. Thus, someone with a strong religious belief was less likely to act only according to his or her personal motivation and always took into consideration the goals of the community. No matter what their culture or their language, the respondents used terms like *tolerance, truthfulness, responsibility,* and *personal honesty* when describing the concepts that they felt made a religion a success.

These findings truly moved me and gave me much hope and encouragement for my work. It seemed to me that the attitudes reflected in this survey laid bare a code of humanity that we all carry within us. It is a code that we can appeal to when we, as an international community, face the challenges of our future. Perhaps this continuing search for our common values, hopes, and dreams is all we really need to help us stay on the difficult road toward global understanding.

Responsibility for Bertelsmann

The Success Story of Corporate Culture

In the year 2010, we celebrated the 175th anniversary of the Bertelsmann publishing house.[60] Few other media conglomerates in the world have such a long tradition and history. Bertelsmann was founded as a Protestant publisher in the first half of the nineteenth century. Its core values of social engagement, providing for employees and their families, civic participation in the headquarters' location, and developing and supporting social services have been an integral part of Bertelsmann since the beginning. In the nineteenth and twentieth centuries, the Bertelsmann and Mohn families founded a school, a kindergarten, and a library in their hometown, and with the creation of retirement benefits and corporate health insurance, they helped define the social principles of corporate responsibility.[61] To be part of this legacy is demanding as well as inspiring.

My husband often talked about his parents and grandparents, and his memories were vivid. His family's Protestant way of thinking had greatly influenced him, and he wanted to build on the things that he had learned as a child. But the volatile history of the twentieth century, and the devastation that National Socialism and World War II brought upon Germany, hit Bertelsmann hard as well. When my husband returned home in January 1946 after being an American prisoner of war, a large part of his hometown—along with his publishing house—was in ruins. His older brother Heinrich had been killed in the war, and his father was very ill. Reinhard was barely twenty-five years old, yet the entire burden of postwar reconstruction lay on his shoulders. Although he was young, he was raised in a tradition of entrepreneurship, and he took on his life's task completely.[62]

In all our conversations, as well as in the hundreds of his notes in our company archives,[63] he was always thinking about his goals and responsibilities as a business leader. As much as he sought to maintain the tradition of corporate responsibility, he was also very unconventional in his support of new ideas, which he saw as necessary to meet the demands of our time and our modern society. In the 1950s, he developed a system—with his head of distribution, Fritz Wixforth—to create one of the world's largest book and distribution businesses through the use of catalogs as well as salesmen to deliver books directly into readers' homes. He then added industry and service sectors. In the 1960s, his was one of the first businesses in Germany to begin to expand internationally.

He never forgot how difficult it was for his business

to get bank loans during the early years of postwar reconstruction. To this day, my children still remember the family vacations when "Tata" suddenly had to get on a plane and leave—usually because there was a problem with the bank and he had to make a case for his capital investment needs. The incredible postwar growth brought many challenges, along with sleepless nights and always new and surprising fears and worries. On the weekends, he would often take hour-long walks outdoors trying to clear his head, or he would talk to me about his worries.

Being at the side of Reinhard Mohn, I learned that even a successful business has its highs and its lows and that mistakes are made. But I also realized that a lot can be learned from difficult experiences. Just as a top team can be a boon for any business, personal disappointments must also be dealt with and overcome.

In the face of constantly growing new obligations, my husband decided, after just a few years of heading the company, that he would not be able to fully manage all of the corporate responsibilities and leadership on his own. If the business was to keep growing, a new leadership structure would have to be developed that could keep pace with the company's rapid expansion. Corporate responsibility and leadership were to be delegated to several creative heads. What seems like standard management structure today was extremely innovative at the time in Germany, for it was a shift from the established patriarchal corporate structure. For this new direction not only meant a surrender of power on the management side; it also put new responsibilities into the hands of the employees, a proposition that was heretofore unknown and caused a great deal of uncertainty.

Suddenly, human resources at Bertelsmann had many new responsibilities: training seminars, consultations, and many time-consuming one-on-one conversations were all part of ushering in this new era. Over the decades, I watched as my husband took part in even the most contentious worker debates. He faced every conflict head-on, because he firmly believed that a company can chart positive growth only if its employees feel connected to their jobs.

As a young man, my husband joined close to one hundred Bertelsmann employees in clearing away the debris and the ruins left after the war, just to be able to get production started again. Working together like this, in the darkest hours, toward a new beginning, led him to an intrinsic understanding of the meaning of partnership. While the unions were skeptical, and the press even called him "Red Mohn," he held steady in his belief that partnership between employer and employee was the most important aspect of corporate leadership. He wanted nothing more than to convince people of this belief, and he always wanted his employees to be on his side.

As I myself have witnessed countless times, employees

can be incredibly creative when given your trust. People who can identify with the goals of their corporation are likely to be more engaged and motivated than are those who feel misunderstood and cannot relate to the objectives of their superiors. The great successes that Bertelsmann enjoyed after the Second World War can largely be ascribed to the corporate culture that my husband developed.[64] The powerful forces of motivation, identification, and creativity that he recognized, developed, and implemented into the company structure are the key to the Bertelsmann success story.

As a global media conglomerate with approximately 100,000 employees in more than fifty countries, Bertelsmann is very aware of the considerable economic, sociopolitical, and social responsibilities that it shoulders. While our worldwide dissemination of information, education, and entertainment makes contributions to society, we also strive for economic success and to be at the top of the market. Yet our objective of capital growth is always connected with the core values of our corporate culture. The goals and values that are summarized in the Bertelsmann Essentials[65] reflect the basic requirements that are needed for any human interaction. A successful partnership is built on mutual trust and the delegation of responsibility. Employees' access to information and the sharing of profits are naturally also part of the equation.

We believe that the connectedness and motivation of

the individual contribute vastly to the creativity, growth, and efficiency of the whole. We ask all employees to fully take advantage of the responsibilities given to them so that they can act from a position of independent leadership. Nevertheless, the key to success lies in decentralization. Our separate firms operate with the greatest possible freedoms. The result of this decentralization is corporate flexibility and commercial efficiency.

This type of corporate freedom, however, demands a commitment on the part of the employee to align with the interests of the company as a whole. Our firm tries to retain the world's top creative minds and entrepreneurial talents. Supporting them and continuously developing their skills ensures corporate continuity. We want to be a harbor for creatives and artists, and we are committed to the protection of intellectual property. Our various programs guarantee a plurality of points of view and opinions, and we fully respect artistic freedom and the freedom of the press. While we advocate democracy and freedom of speech all over the world, we also respect the traditions and values of the countries in which we are active.

At the center of all our business transactions is the customer. It's for him or her that we develop our products and services, and our ongoing success stems from our focus on the customer combined with a continued willingness to innovate. Among all our different businesses, a strict adherence to law and justice, to upholding the highest ethical standards, and to opposing discrimination and harassment at the workplace is our biggest imperative. We expect our coworkers to act with utmost responsibility for their colleagues as well as for their society and their environment. We trust that our endeavors as publishers and as entrepreneurs will bear results that are beneficial to the general public, and we acknowledge our unique responsibility toward our society.

In order to safeguard our company's independence and continuity, the Bertelsmann Foundation remains our majority shareholder. My husband's credo was always "With ownership comes responsibility." To honor this principle, he founded the Bertelsmann Foundation in 1977. Its goal was to bring new energy to what he thought was badly needed reform in Germany. Since the 1970s, he had been dissatisfied with his nation's performance in many areas. Following Germany's "economic miracle," and after numerous social reforms, a certain inflexibility had settled upon the country, which my husband thought was dangerous. In his opinion, a community can remain viable only if its citizens are able to identify with the goals of the state, then develop a sense of personal responsibility for the greater good. In return, citizens expect transparency from their government and want to be able to understand the motivations behind political decisions. Therefore our social goals and political decisions must always be examined, and the results must be measurable and subject to appraisal.

Such a measure of performance, as my husband imagined it, would be based upon a close comparison with other countries and other organizations. With its political, economic, and public projects, the fully operational Bertelsmann Foundation supports the continued development of our democratic systems and builds models for bringing positive change to our society's structures and institutions.[66]

Leadership in Responsibility

After my husband's death in October 2009, a large responsibility for the house of Bertelsmann was transferred to me, which I have taken on with pride and joy. I can negotiate these many responsibilities only with the support of my family, input from trustworthy advisers, and my own personal perseverance.

I am the speaker of the family and the chair of the executive board of the Bertelsmann Management Company (BVG), which controls all voting rights at the annual general meeting of Bertelsmann AG. The executive board's responsibilities include overseeing the interests of the two shareholder groups, the Bertelsmann Foundation and the Bertelsmann family, as well as protecting the corporate continuity and culture at Bertelsmann. The steering committee, which I head, includes as its members my children Brigitte and Christoph, who support me greatly. They share the same goal that I have: to ensure the autonomy of Bertelsmann AG for the long term. In addition, there are three managers at my side at BVG whom I can depend on at any time: Dieter H.

Vogel, Dr. Jürgen Strube, and Dr. Werner J. Bauer. With a board like this, the house of Bertelsmann is in excellent hands. I will make the decision about who will succeed me as the family representative at a later date.

As a member of the supervisory board of Bertelsmann AG, and especially of the staff committee, one of my main concerns is that Bertelsmann retain its partnership-based corporate culture. During my visits to firms all over the world, one thing always stood out for me: companies that seek out a partner-based dialogue with their employees, that grant their leadership entrepreneurial autonomy, and that include everyone in the sharing of corporate success can truly prosper in the international market. It is thus critical that any new executives are a good fit with our company's corporate culture. Our supervisory board is made up of renowned leaders from large international corporations, who do an excellent job of supporting and supervising the executive board. I am very happy that as members of the executive board Brigitte and Christoph are also by my side and that they share in the responsibility for Bertelsmann AG. Lastly, the operations of the business are carried out by a six-person board.

I am especially pleased to continue the tradition of social engagement that has always been so valued by the Bertelsmann and Mohn families. As vice chair of the Bertelsmann Foundation's executive board and as a member of the board of trustees, I have a great deal of input into shaping the direction of the charitable Bertelsmann Foundation. My daughter, Brigitte, who is responsible for the health and society programs of the foundation, is also a member of its executive board. My son Christoph now shoulders his own share of social responsibility as a member of the board of trustees of the Bertelsmann Foundation, and as the chairman of the board of the newly founded Reinhard Mohn Foundation.

There is always much discussion in our family about the foundation's work. Whenever possible, we meet on Sundays for a family meal. Lively conversations about our various responsibilities are naturally a big part of these get-togethers. Our children never knew the separation of work and family life that is so common in most families. Just because it's the weekend, you simply cannot leave behind your obligations to a company like Bertelsmann or to a foundation as large as ours.

My responsibilities at Bertelsmann include dealing with content, answering strategic challenges, and using sound human judgment. Every person in a leadership position develops their own leadership style. While working at Bertelsmann, I learned that without strict self-discipline, my workload is simply not manageable. I stay in shape by swimming, running, and maintaining a healthy diet. And I am continuously in contact with any colleagues who are leading projects on their own.

Without delegating responsibilities, this amount of

work would simply not be doable. I am in favor of a vital and multifaceted working environment that enables open and constructive discussions. It is easy to have an exchange of ideas with those who share your opinion, but it is much more enriching when other perspectives are heard. Whenever I speak with our executives and other colleagues, I listen very carefully to everyone's opinion without letting my own judgment be known. Only in this way can I be sure that the person I am speaking to is honest and open with me and is not hiding their real opinion.

There is no such thing as a working life without conflict. Over the years I have learned that fact-based conflicts can best be solved when the differing opinions are openly discussed. It is important to recognize that we all make mistakes, but we can learn from these mistakes. Mistakes must be forgiven. If something goes wrong, the problem is put out on the table. After that, everyone can look into one another's eyes, and energy isn't wasted on unresolved conflicts. Incidentally, this strategy does not just apply to company life. It is just as valid for life with a partner and for our relationships with children and friends. Only by facing challenges can you live a life of conviction.

Leading people is a big challenge. Each of us has our own way, our own needs, and our own motivations. In the end, each employee decides for him- or herself what to do and what not to do, along with the when and the how. Leaders must recognize this, because they are ultimately responsible for the work of all the employees.

A successful leader places the individual at the center. A large part of my working day is taken up with dialogues with our executives, exchanges with our colleagues, and discussions with business leaders, experts, and scientists. Having a conversation as equal partners is extremely valuable, for the best ideas are often formed during a discussion. The more difficult it is to make a decision, the more time I spend engaged in deep conversations and reflections.

As much as I sometimes like to make spontaneous decisions, there is no room for spontaneity when it comes to dealing with larger issues. It is very important to me that all opinions be heard during a debate and that sides are not taken too quickly. I learned from my husband that carefully considering pros and cons and giving undivided thought to often highly complex issues are some of the most integral skills of corporate responsibility. Behind every success are long stretches of hard work and sometimes painful decisions that can cost a lot of energy. Sleepless nights, too, are part of the journey. If my nerves are on edge and the tension is just too much, it is time to take a break. The awareness of how much responsibility

I have is always there. In a company of our size, at any time during a vacation, on a weekend, or on a holiday, an unforeseen event can happen or a decision must be made.

"Do everything with consultation, and you will have no regrets when the deed is done."[67] This saying by Saint Benedict has become my life's motto. So far, it has served me well. In my over forty years of working, I have learned that the process for making decisions must be given highest priority. And in a highly complex decision-making process, there is no one right decision. Instead, there are often many different solutions, each with its own pluses and minuses.

A number of studies have now confirmed my personal experience that the use of reason is not enough for avoiding mistakes.[68] The human brain is not a calculator. The psychoanalyst Sigmund Freud was one of the first to discover that our subconscious has a huge influence on our decision-making process.

I am very interested in this process and have sought out many conversations with leading neuroscientists. Scientists estimate that human consciousness, which is concentrated on the left side of the brain, can process about forty units of information per second. The unconscious mind, on the other hand, which operates mostly at the rear of the right side, can process 15 to 20 million units per second. With such a huge amount of information, it is no surprise that subconscious thinking is vague and lacks detail. But if we were to actually wait and consciously gather all the facts that are available on an issue, we would surely never arrive at a result.

Modern research has discovered that the brain collects all our experiences and uses them as an emotional reservoir. It is from these experiences that we recognize mistakes, learn from them, and try to avoid them in the future. Especially in leadership positions, when we are faced with an unlimited array of choices, our emotional reservoirs will send out signals that can ease our decision-making process. These are the so-called somatic markers.[69] The emotional part of the brain is just as much a part of the decision-making process as the rational part of the brain. My gut instinct often leads me to the right decision, as I've later confirmed by comparing information and considering expert opinions. I am convinced that factoring in one's feelings is the right thing to do when making decisions. Gerd Gigerenzer, one of the most renowned researchers on heuristics and decision making, who is now director of the Max Planck Institute for Human Development, told me that there are numerous situations in which it's best to trust your instincts.[70]

Of course, personal feelings alone are not enough for making responsible decisions. After a first intuitive reaction, common sense must set in to evaluate its meaning and assess it in terms of the impending decision. To me, a heightened awareness and presence of mind is, however, a key factor in responsible leadership. In many cases, a reconciliation between the subconscious and reason occurs surprisingly fast. Whoever uses their well of emotional experience, and in the course of their working years puts it to the test, will become more decisive and more secure, sometimes able to evaluate a situation in mere seconds. Personally, I can say that my best decisions have always been those where common sense and intuition see eye to eye.

Yet there will always be challenges where all our experiences won't help. Sometimes, no matter what, we simply can't come up with a solution, and our thoughts run in circles. A situation like this can be paralyzing; it can block decisions and weaken our creative strengths. I have learned to quickly put an end to these situations by obtaining expert advice and taking into account the opinions of others.

Anyone who is responsible for others must earn their trust. This means setting a personal example, having an open discourse, enabling transparency in decision making, and naming clear goals. It is especially important to examine one's own actions. Am I doing the right thing? Or is there another, perhaps better, way? I question myself more than anyone else, and I always seek discourse with proven experts.

Yet I am also aware of the value of emotions. You have to carry people along, even—and especially—during times of difficult changes. I personally think one-on-one conversations are very valuable. Besides our meetings and conferences, I always find time to meet with our leading managers in private. This does not just apply to my responsibilities as a member of the executive board and the board of trustees of the Bertelsmann Foundation, or to my seats on the supervisory board or staff committee of Bertelsmann AG. In conjunction with our human resource manager, I am always on the lookout for talented young leadership, and I try to uncover the unique potentials of our new colleagues. On occasion, the supervisory board will invite young leadership to a dinner, giving our newest staff an opportunity to present themselves. Seeing everyone's unique talents and immense expertise gives me great joy and motivation.

Business leaders must never pursue only their financial goals. They must also be sensitive to human needs. Every coworker is part of the mosaic that makes up the company. If a corporation's culture encourages mutual trust, it will fuel a great deal of creativity and commitment. If, however, individual employees feel that their work is not valued, or if they fear for their positions, they will lose their drive, they will be blocked by fear, and they will never achieve as much as those who feel protected and are motivated to give their best.

Part of our corporate tradition is taking into account the sustainability of our efforts. The history of a

175-year-old firm is never one of just highlights. Crises are averted, lean times are overcome, mistakes are made, and things that have become dear are cast aside in order to try new things. If you want to try something new, you may have to take two steps back. Or three, or four. Every learning process has its share of ups and downs. I learned from my husband that the tireless search for new ways and solutions often leads to pleasantly surprising results. He had the uncanny ability to combine unconventional ideas with the traditions of the house of Bertelsmann. This is the standard I will always hold myself to.

The Future of Corporate Culture

The underlying values of our corporate culture, the so-called Bertelsmann Essentials,[71] are binding for shareholders, as well as for executives and coworkers. Our work is specifically guided by the values of partnership, corporate freedom, creativity, and social responsibility. Someone might say, "That's just lip service." But lip service is worthless. The meaningfulness of our corporate culture arises from its daily implementation: from the culture of togetherness that informs our day-to-day business, and that in the end makes it tangible and concrete. To achieve it, many tools were developed over several decades at Bertelsmann.

Our company's corporate culture places much emphasis on dialogue with our coworkers. But how can you engage in a dialogue with more than 100,000 people? To do so, Bertelsmann developed its employee survey, the first one in 1977 in Germany, and it has been used internationally since 2002. Every four years the company's employees hand in a detailed evaluation of their superiors, their working environment, and their firm. In

2010, about 85 percent of all employees worldwide participated in the last survey. In 2006, participation was equally high.

These numbers confirm the extraordinarily wide acceptance of this tool. The survey results are an important indicator of the state of our company and are thus taken very seriously by our management. In addition, the ongoing dialogue between leadership and employees is crucial for maintaining a partnership-based working environment. A feeling of personal worth is a big motivating factor. For giving personal feedback, we have developed a number of very specific tools. These conversations follow mandatory guidelines that were established for management.[72] Everyone in a leadership position at Bertelsmann must follow these guiding principles. The main purpose of these personal conversations is the continued development, both professional and personal, of the employee; they also define his or her health care support. We consider the training and continuing education of our coworkers to be a significant contributing factor to the future success of our company.

Another important component of our partner-based corporate leadership is profit sharing with our coworkers. Material equality is a prerequisite for creating worker identification with a company. Commissions destroy any real partnership. So in 1970 my husband introduced the model of profit sharing to Bertelsmann. Bertelsmann AG became one of Germany's originators of profit sharing—it was a groundbreaking pioneer.[73] Over the last forty years, this model has been continually developed. Since the introduction of profit sharing, the company has distributed more than one billion euros net to its employees.[74] Giving only lip service to the concept of corporate culture would look quite different.

These examples are only a small part of our company's day-to-day life. The values that we have posited are constantly being put to the test. Our principles ensure coworkers that they have the right to participate in the decision-making process and thus have a substantial influence on the company's future.

But a corporation is not just made up of noble goals and ideals. Even Bertelsmann can't survive without financial success. But how does the corporate culture contribute to such success? How can we be so sure that our corporate culture not only implements the right values to create a partnership-based working environment, but is also a major contributor to its financial success?

This is a question that business leaders around the world are thinking about. Much research has been done on it. Bertelsmann has commissioned its own very detailed and thorough studies, which are supported by precise data. Our periodic employee surveys shed light on our coworkers' attitudes about their workplace. Through these surveys, we can ascertain whether our employees identify with their responsibilities and whether they are satisfied. At the same time, we can analyze our corporate conditions and the de facto staff performance, for example, by looking at the number of resignations or sick days. Then we can compare these data with the financial success of each of our firms. Our analysis of the relationship between corporate culture and financial success came to the following conclusions:[75]

Clear-cut partner-based leadership goes hand in hand with a strong identification by the coworkers with their tasks and their firm. The extent of this identification is closely tied to the company's financial success. Conversely, the financial success of a company has a strong positive influence on its corporate culture.

Strong employee identification with the workplace promotes productivity as well as worker health. A highly developed corporate culture is evident by fewer numbers of sick days and a comparably low rate of resignation. We compared firms that have a less developed corporate culture to top-ranking companies with the most developed corporate cultures. The result of this comparison showed that poorly led corporations have about two-thirds more resignations and twice as many sick days.

A strong corporate culture has a positive impact on financial success. Employees who are engaged and motivated do not just contribute to a company's success in the short term. The financial impact of the corporate culture becomes especially evident when tracking a firm's economic development over a long period of time. The success rate of companies that have a well-developed corporate culture is twice as high as that of companies with weak corporate cultures. In addition, during the time frame of the study, improving corporate culture led to a growth in financial success.

Our advocacy for corporate culture is more than just lip service. It is also more than just a "soft skill" that can easily be abandoned. At Bertelsmann, corporate culture is a major performance indicator.

A lot of companies consider corporate culture to be a pretty flower, an indulgence you can afford during times of economic growth, but something you would quickly abandon during a financial crisis. But actually the opposite is true. The economic crisis of the last years has shown what a strong corporate culture can accomplish. At Bertelsmann, we, too, were surprised by the extent of the economic crisis. The decline of all the markets pulled the rug out from under many corporations. Like all other companies, we were forced to take drastic cost-reduction measures. Many businessmen and executives told me that they had never experienced such a challenging time— it was the biggest economic crisis in eighty years. What was there to rely on, when everything was collapsing, and when planning became more and more difficult because nobody knew what things would look like in six months, in ten months, or in two years? What would we base our decisions on if everyone was fishing in murky waters? What would we orient ourselves by? My common sense and my intuition both gave me only one answer: our values. Trust in our collective work.

Bertelsmann has seen a lot of crises in its 175-year history. It survived two world wars. We faced great challenges during the oil crises of the 1970s and the world financial crisis that began in the late 1980s in the United States and reached Germany in the early 1990s.[76] The breakdown of the new economy at the beginning of this century cost us dearly. Yet all our efforts were always geared toward the future. At the same time, we never lost sight of the basic values of our corporate culture. They are the building blocks of our stability and our confidence.

Bertelsmann's very clear ownership structure accounts for its continuity and dependability. Our management, as well as our employees, know exactly what the shareholders' values are. Our employees know that the owners are looking toward the company's long-term development and security, and that they would not be tempted to make premature decisions for short-term capital gains. Bertelsmann is independent and can operate autonomously. This, too, gives management greater freedom. It's no secret that a few years ago Bertelsmann bought back 25 percent of its shares for 4.5 billion euros from the Belgian group Bruxelles Lambert. I would like to take this opportunity to say in plain language: my family and I are not enemies of the stock market. But we believe in self-determination.

Naturally, good and bad decisions are made in every company, whether it is listed on the stock market or privately held. But corporate leadership will more likely decide in favor of company continuity and will more likely align its goals with the good of the workforce if responsible owners are in charge of corporate strategies. This has been proven internationally. The most recent crisis demonstrated that Bertelsmann is well equipped, even if the world's economy gets into rough waters. Our values are what make Bertelsmann a predictable and reliable partner. Our coworkers, as well as our clients, business partners, and society as a whole know that they can rely on us. Our reliability during even the most difficult times creates confidence, which in today's difficult times has become a valuable commodity. I am convinced that the value-based system that we practice daily can set an example for our society, for our politicians, and for other commercial enterprises.

The Future Concerns Us All

There Is No Such Thing as a Democracy Without Values and Trust

A psychological study that the Bertelsmann Foundation carried out at the end of 2010[77] showed that Germans are skeptical about the prospects for their future. After the financial crises of 2008 and 2009, 70 percent of those surveyed have lost all confidence in their institutions, decision makers, and other policy makers. Social safety systems are distrusted as well. Almost half of all those surveyed would like a system change in terms of our market economy and our democracy.

These results are alarming. Many of our citizens feel resigned and have little faith in the continued development of Germany or in their future quality of life.

The cause for this drop in confidence seems initially to be recent developments on the international financial markets, along with political developments in Germany. But seen from a historical standpoint, this loss of confidence is the result not only of the current economic crisis but of a long-standing, underestimated development. Those surveyed said that the most meaningful ways of social interaction occurred during the 1960s and 1970s, which can best be described as "wealth through growth." Looking back, the respondents assigned the decision makers of the 1960s a much higher degree of competence and believability than those of today. They associated the 1990s with an increase in the growth of the power elite and a decrease in the representation of citizens' interests. They felt that social inequality as a result of globalization has been quietly tolerated for much too long.

Those who were surveyed also connected present difficulties to false promises made by those in finance and politics. Our time now is considered to be marked by a profit-driven robbery of man and his environment; unchecked egotism is triumphing over shared values and goals.

All in all, the recent financial crisis marks a low point, and many citizens have a critical view of the future. Today's policy makers in finance and politics are mostly accused of greed and of following the interests of lobbies, and of being out of touch with reality. The respondents also criticized the insufficient breakdown of bureaucratic hurdles and the strict adherence to tradition.

In the next years, those surveyed are hoping for the return to guaranteed basic security for all people. But these hopes are vague, and the mood in this country reflects the growing disparity in our society. This is quite alarming. Germany was once a nation of progress. One of the great postwar promises was that all people in this country, no matter what their social class, would have more education, more wealth, and greater acceptance available to them. The idea that social advancement was possible for all people was the driving force behind life in West Germany. The middle class of our society had become transparent. The view of West German society for decades had always been a view to the top. Things were supposed to get better and better, and they did—at least for a while.

The optimism that carried our society forward for so long is now gone. Attitudes have become abrasive. The shared hope that things would get better has been shattered. The economy of globalization has created winners and losers, and our society is starting to fall apart.

Studies show that people who grow up in socially and economically disadvantaged households have only a small chance of attaining a better standard of living.[78] In numerous studies, the Bertelsmann Foundation has pointed out that Germany's educational system does not adequately nurture children from socially and economically disadvantaged families. If Germany is to overcome its challenges, it must set goals that are sustainable over the long run and make decisive investments into its education and training systems. Our country has few commodities, and education is the only resource upon which we can build our future.[79]

For a number of years now, the Bertelsmann Foundation has pointed out the challenges of integrating foreign citizens into our community. The income discrepancy, too, can become a point of conflict. It has become much more difficult for people in this country to overcome social boundaries or to climb up the social or economic ladder. Many people believe that their own children will not be able to sustain the standard of living that they currently have. The fight for status is creating a new dog-eat-dog mentality that is causing the members of our society to drift further and further apart. Many more people are losing social status than are gaining it.[80] Such a development is very dangerous. When the chances of moving up and the risks of moving down are no longer equally weighted, our performance-based society loses its balance. If there is nothing to be gained by working, there is no more motivation to work. The result will be a lowering of performance and, finally, a loss of prosperity.

For decades, the citizens of Germany believed that the building blocks of life consisted of going to school, perhaps attending university, getting a job, moving up, starting a family, and building a house. But the reality today is different. A contemporary labor market study that the Bertelsmann Foundation published in January 2010 in conjunction with the Institute for the Study of Labor indicates that since the year 2001 traditional working conditions in Germany have greatly declined in comparison

Mikhail Gorbachev, former president of the Soviet Union, a guest of the Bertelsmann Foundation with Reinhard and Liz Mohn (1992).

Liz and Reinhard Mohn with Jerusalem mayor Teddy Kollek (1993).

German president Johannes Rau with his wife, Christina, at the ceremony for the twenty-fifth anniversary of the Bertelsmann Foundation (2002).

At the Salzburg Trilogue with Austrian chancellor Dr. Wolfgang Schüssel (2005).

The Bertelsmann Foundation's cultural forum in New Delhi: Liz Mohn and Sonia Gandhi, president of the Indian National Congress (2005).

Lower Saxony Premier Christian Wulff led discussions at the Bertelsmann Foundation (2006).

Liz Mohn with the former U.S. secretary of state Dr. Henry Kissinger at the Global Policy Council in Berlin (2009).

Former UN secretary-general Kofi Annan presents the Vernon A. Walters Award of the Atlantik-Brücke nonprofit organization to Liz Mohn, the first woman to receive the prestigious award (2008).

Ambassadors for the Bertelsmann Foundation's "Integration Through Education" campaign, "All Kids Are VIPs": Liz Mohn (center); Dr. Gunter Thielen, chairman of the Bertelsmann Foundation executive board; and minister of state Dr. Maria Böhmer (2008).

At the launch of the Liz Mohn Culture and Music Foundation, with the Gütersloh Boys' Choir and their artistic director, Sigmund Bothmann (2007).

Liz Mohn and Gütersloh's mayor Maria Unger in the daycare center "Die Lütken" with the winners of the Liz Mohn Culture and Music Foundation's initiative "Integration Through Music" (2009).

Women as management forces gain strength: Liz Mohn with the Business Women School of the Bertelsmann Foundation at Schloss Ziethen (2010).

Dr. Gunter Thielen, chairman of the board of the Bertelsmann Foundation, as a guest of the Business Women School; he supports Liz Mohn's initiatives (2010).

Liz Mohn receives a kiss on the hand from star conductor Herbert von Karajan on the 150th anniversary of Bertelsmann AG in Gütersloh (1985).

With Munich director and conductor August Everding as jury chairman at the Bertelsmann Foundation's international singing competition "New Voices" (1995).

Liz Mohn and Gustav Kuhn, artistic director of the international singing competition "New Voices," with Sir Peter Ustinov (right), the jury's honorary chairman (2001).

South Korea takes the top three spots: the winners of "New Voices 2009"are (from left) Kihwan Sim, Eunju Kwon (first place), and JunHo You, pictured here with Liz Mohn and Dominique Meyer (center), jury chairman and designated director of the Viennese state opera.

With Eva Luise Köhler, the wife of the German president, working together for the German Stroke Aid Foundation (2008).

Liz Mohn and Max Ackermann, children's ambassador of the German Stroke Aid Foundation, at a press conference supporting "15 Years Against Stroke" (2008).

Reinhard and Liz Mohn in the foyer of the Bertelsmann Foundation (2008).

At the opening of the Reinhard Mohn Institute at the University of Witten-Herdecke: Liz Mohn with son Christoph Mohn and daughter Dr. Brigitte Mohn (2010).

The first ceremony of the Reinhard Mohn Prize: German chancellor Angela Merkel gave the keynote address (2011).

with other nations.[81] While in industry traditional labor models still dominate, the service industry has seen a decline. Today 53.2 percent of workers in Germany—that is, only about every second person—are working full-time and without a time limit on their employment. There's no doubt about it: our labor market is reacting to an increasing demand for flexibility by cutting back on traditional employment models. The market is taking advantage of the alternative employment models created by our political system. The social consequences cannot yet be predicted.

The life stories of working Germans have become fractured. How can young people plan their lives, find a partner, and start a family if they are employed on only a fixed-term basis? In addition, the decline of traditional working conditions is in no way gender neutral. Between 2001 and 2008, the percentage of women who are employed in traditional work dropped from 48 to around 43 percent. Among the twenty-eight OECD countries that were evaluated, Germany had the lowest percentage after the Netherlands and Switzerland. Traditional work structures have decreased to a greater extent for women than for men.

The increased employment for women was largely due to temporary work. But unstable employment creates unstable lives. It creates a weaker society, it lessens the engagement by the individual in social issues, it prevents a whole generation from creating and holding together families, and it weakens the social contract that is still the basis of a free and democratic society. A democracy without shared values and social convictions cannot survive.[82] This is a challenge for both government and the finance sector. The increase in unstable working conditions is not just an economic issue—it is also a political issue, and it creates political problems. I thus appeal to all businesses to acknowledge their responsibility to our society. The experiences at Bertelsmann gave us all hope that a corporate culture can indeed plant the seed for new values, like respect for others, partnerships, and mutual trust, which can be learned as early as in kindergarten.[83]

A society that is prepared for the future is everyone's concern! Anyone who is in a position of responsibility, or who wants to be, has a challenge. The longer we remain silent, the more rigid our society will become. We all have to show our colors and articulate what is important to us. Only through an open dialogue and only by sharing our common values can our society regain its strength and optimism.

In November 2009 the Bertelsmann Foundation published a study that clearly indicated that the economic crisis had left indelible marks on the conscience of Germans. For many Germans, personal relationships, marriage, family, partnerships, and friends have become important since the financial crisis.[84] The search for meaning and direction, too, has intensified for many. At the same time, people want material security. A lot of people hope that the current crisis will eventually lead to less discrepancy between rich and poor, to more solidarity between young and old, and to a more positive assimilation of immigrants. Nevertheless, many also doubt that the crisis will actually result in a more cohesive community, or will cause large businesses to rethink their policies. Only one-third of the respondents believe that the economy will realign itself with long-term material welfare more than with short-term profits. But despite all skepticism, a large majority in Germany wishes for the crisis to result in a more cohesive society. This wish should be our guide into the future!

Today's economy and the way we live are threats to our natural resources. They are also threats to international cohesion and to the worldwide trust in politics and economics. The economic crisis has demonstrated that we need long-term strategies to improve and maintain the quality of life, for ourselves and for future generations. We all must work toward sustainability. Forty-nine percent of people in Germany believe that the economic crisis has brought about an ecological reevaluation. Government policy should take advantage of this potential toward solidarity in both ecological and social issues.

Each of us can become an example for others by following our personal convictions and principles. Every new dialogue can create a bridge across our current social inflexibility. We cannot lose ourselves. Everybody can make a personal contribution, so that things will soon go upward again. In the international dialogue, too, Germany must maintain its credibility.

Reliability creates trust. The path of Bertelsmann proves that this trust can also contribute to financial success.

On the Social Responsibility
of Businesses

Corporations are part of our society. But without a well-functioning social environment, a company cannot financially survive. A country's prosperity stems from the success of its competitive businesses. But the state-sponsored security that until now has been provided to corporations has reached its limit in today's globalized and financially interdependent world. The old mechanisms don't work anymore. This is why there are discussions around the world about "corporate social responsibility"— the responsibility that large corporations have for their society. Smaller and midsize corporations as well can no longer dodge the issue of their social responsibility.[85]

What does corporate social responsibility mean, and how is it to be taken on? It means contributing to the well-being of a society by acting above and beyond its legal obligations. It means laying claim to responsibility by coordinating its value creation processes with ecological and social parameters, and by making a commitment to the design of its social environment.

The social responsibility of a company is not a one-way street. Both the company and society stand to profit:

Good working conditions foster employee motivation.

The responsible use of resources leads to sustained viability for the company.

A well-functioning infrastructure secures long-term competitiveness.

Fair practice in product creation supports trust and improves the life and working conditions in developing and threshold countries.

A commitment to social and cultural initiatives promotes stature and trust in business transactions.

Of course, corporate action cannot replace political action. It can, however, be a meaningful addition to politics. With this in mind, it is interesting to note that eight of the ten richest countries in the world, measured according to gross national product, are functioning democracies.[86] All available investigations point out that countries with a functioning democracy have a higher economic performance, possess a better infrastructure, and offer a higher measure of internal and outside security than nondemocratic nations.[87] If our society wants to be ready for the future, then responsibilities for politics and economy must be redistributed. We cannot meet the constant pressure on our social and educational systems to reform without the involvement of all the players and without the close cooperation among all the social policy decision makers. While the decision-making processes and the plans for action may differ among the various players, goals that create commonalities such as sustainability, social responsibility, education support, and family-friendliness should supply the necessary target orientation for all those involved.

The Bertelsmann Foundation is fully committed to these goals on the local, regional, and international levels. On a local level, we work to initiate the cooperation between social organizations and commercial enterprises. On a regional level, we support the creation of a network that connects businesses, politics, and the community so that they can jointly develop solutions for pressing regional problems, like business locations, lack of skilled labor, lack of social cohesion, or environmental challenges. The regions are supported by a nationwide initiatives group, which is made up of well-known businesses that have recognized that assuming responsibility for one's society is an irrefutable part of their commercial activities.

Many companies are now represented worldwide and maintain production sites all over the world. They must coordinate deliveries with suppliers and manage the sale of the product on the world market across many continents. Businesses that are internationally active are often presented with diverse issues, especially in developing and emerging countries. Poverty, a lack of adequate medical care, and education deficits are often part of daily life there. The players on the global market now have a unique task ahead of them, especially because in these countries the local governmental institutions are often strained. The amount of social responsibility that a corporation is willing to take on is a deciding factor for creating a fair plan for globalization. The benefit of this type of involvement is not just the securing of the respective markets. Businesses have the opportunity to actively participate in creating a balance between rich and poor and securing long-term peace in a globalized world.

Compared to other countries, in Germany the encouraging successes at the international as well as the regional level are unfortunately still barely taught in universities. This is especially regrettable, because conforming company projects efficiently and effectively to the guidelines of corporate social responsibility places high demands on management. Expert knowledge is indispensable. For this reason, a greater commitment to corporate social responsibility in higher education and training is especially important. The students of today are the future of our society. The Bertelsmann Foundation has launched a number of pilot seminars at various German universities to introduce the concept of "social responsibility" to economics and business administration students.[88] Real-world examples are used to demonstrate the possibilities of social engagement that are available to a corporation, and to show how corporate and economic ethics can be a key to the future success of our society.

Combining Family and Work

On my many trips I have noticed again and again that women in other countries are often much better able to negotiate the split between work and family life than are women in Germany. Committed women in France, for example, have no doubt that working and family can be combined. Internationally, Germany is clearly behind in this aspect.

In the coming decades, a more successful combination of work and family is one of the great challenges for German society. We call upon economic and government policy to create better conditions for a successful work-life balance.[89] Demographic changes and the increase in single households are part of today's reality.[90] On average in Germany, every third marriage ends in divorce, and in urban centers, it is every second marriage. Our birthrate stands at 1.35 children per woman—very few countries have so few children being born. Germany has the highest rate of couples without children. About a third of the population will not have children, and the number of women of childbearing age is at a steady decline. A family with several children is more and more becoming the exception to the rule. Every third child under five years old does not have any siblings. Last, the more educated the parents are, the fewer children they have.

For Germany as well as for Europe, this is an alarming development. We face not only the challenges of a childless society, but also a society that is aging. This demographic change is fully in effect, yet without children our society has no future. Combined with the effects of globalization, family-friendliness is an important location factor that is not to be underestimated for German and European businesses.

The desire for children, especially among men, is still steadily declining. But, in complete opposition to our demographic development, according to the Fifteenth Shell Youth Study undertaken in 2006, more than 70 percent of youth state that a family is necessary to live a happy life.[91] And 85 percent of children in Germany have grown up within a family.[92]

There is no question: our society is marked by contradictions. We have not yet been able to dismantle these contradictions and find a direction that combines all our wishes and needs. But the examples of other countries may be a guide. Both France and the Scandinavian countries have proven that it is indeed possible to have a positive impact on demographic development. Systematic support for families and for combining work and family life leads to consistent or even growing birthrates. But no matter what the solutions we eventually adopt, examining the big picture from all sides is essential. A main focus will be to make concrete improvements in the lives of parents who are part of the modern workforce. We need to ask what the state can tangibly do for mothers, fathers, and children. It is also important to set up parameters within which government and business can help families. It is dearly important to me to set in motion ideas and initiatives that can direct us to a way out of Germany's dilemma.

To this end, the Bertelsmann Foundation held a symposium in 2007 in Berlin that compared the work-life balances across Europe.[93] We specifically looked across borders, highlighted some marked developments in European OECD countries, and presented the latest research results. Some very successful real-life examples were presented, demonstrating that a combination of work and daily life is certainly possible, as long as businesses have the courage to lead by example.

At Bertelsmann we are aware that family-oriented staff policies must be a part of our partnership-based corporate culture. It is unrealistic to believe that private and professional lives can be strictly separated. Employees bring their problems from home to the workplace, and conversely they take their work problems home to the family. Work-life balance is simply part of any partnership-based corporate culture. From its many studies, Bertelsmann has learned that women who have part-time jobs are sick less often than women who only take care of the home and family. The reconciliation of work and family can therefore also lead to greater self-confidence and is thus an excellent foundation for having healthy and motivated male and female workers.[94]

To support the reconciliation of family and work, we have introduced a number of incentives at our various company locations. These include:

- flexible working hours
- day care for children under three
- a family service for emergencies
- a parent-child room for emergencies
- vacation programs for children, to relieve the parents

We know that being successful at work leads to personal satisfaction. Conversely, family is a resource for professional strength. I am convinced that the corporate culture at Bertelsmann—with its freedoms, its delegation of responsibilities, the possibility of independently organized and self-determined tasks, as well as its project- and team-based management style—has created flexible solutions and family-friendly work models for many of our employees. Still, not all of life's dreams can be fulfilled at the same time. Especially those in leadership positions will always be walking a fine line, and there will always be a demand for creative solutions. A constant presence will always be required of our executives. Working part-time in this capacity can become a dead end for ambitious women. Yet women still have to learn to view their career trajectory as a marathon.

Many women find it especially hard to accept setbacks and defeats. But herein lies the secret to success. Women, too, must learn from their mistakes, get back up after a defeat, and develop staying power during difficult phases. In my experience, having the courage to continue even after setbacks is one of the most important requirements for long-term professional success! And having satisfaction at work gives women self-confidence.

In order to have a career and a family life at the same time, you have to learn to let go. Many women find it difficult to hand over responsibility. But that is exactly what it takes to manage all our daily responsibilities. Women must learn to delegate without having a guilty conscience, because no matter how disciplined we are, we cannot do it all. Striving for perfection can make you sick. If you place high demands on yourself, you must watch your health and try to remain open to criticism. It is during my conversations with others that I learn the most about my own potential and my boundaries, and I am able to realistically assess myself.

Family is the most valuable thing we as human beings can experience. Qualities like trust, reliability, warmth, and security are priceless. Most people experience these things only within their families.

A society without children is doomed to failure. It will fail on a social level, because families and their values are what hold our society together. But it will also fail on an emotional level, because family is the place where care, love, and responsibility have their roots. Children create meaning and fulfillment, because they focus our attention onto those things in life that are truly important: to give love, to be there for someone, to live as a community, and to take personal responsibility. It is the duty of our society to create an environment where children and families can have a good life.

For much too long in Germany, economic and family interests were considered to be in opposition. A look at our neighboring countries shows that those with family-friendly infrastructures and family-sensitive working configurations have a considerable increase in financial opportunities. All of us—parents and children, government and society, businesses and the economy— can profit from a healthy balance of family and work.

In order to move one step closer to this goal, I created the Alliance for the Family in 2003 with the minster for family affairs, Renate Schmidt.[95] The members of this alliance, the German Federal Ministry for Family,

Seniors, Women, and Youth, along with the Bertelsmann Foundation and other significant partners, worked to make family-friendliness a hallmark of the German economy. Trade associations and unions, large foundations and leading businesses, as well as government and economic decision makers, all gave their commitment to our goals, provided concrete, practical strategies, and showed us how the work-life balance in our society could be more successful.

I am certain that this path will change our daily lives, step by step. The time has come for a modern and long-term family policy, a policy that aligns its framework for a work-family balance to the realities of the twenty-first century, and that orients itself not along traditional family roles but along the wishes of the people.

Global competition has changed working conditions for many. We must take a hard look at our reality and create a sustainable equilibrium between the needs of the economy and a work-life balance for mothers and fathers. It will then become much easier for people to decide to have children again. The changing mentality in Germany can already be felt!

Many people are looking at the question of creating a work-life balance. In our Alliance for the Family, an international study showed that since 2003 in Germany interest in this subject has steadily increased in all media.[96] The same goes for the Internet. And although the day-care spots for children in Germany cost less than they do in Scandinavia and France, almost everywhere in this country there are not enough. Germany still suffers from a lack of services that are both close to home and able to help relieve household obligations. The women to whom we spoke in our survey still rely on their own networks for child care and other services. And daily life with children is still mostly organized and managed by mothers alone. A work-life balance must become the standard in Germany without creating double burdens. Based on my own experience, it is important to me that women lead a self-determined life and at the same time live with a partner and have a family.

The desire for a family has been well documented in surveys and in the media. But we have a long way to go before making that wish a reality, for concrete actions are required to create the necessary structural change in society. Only lively and strong families and a competitive economy can secure the future of our society. The theme of family concerns us all. We must all contribute if Germany is to once again become a country with a sustainable future.

Women in Leadership Positions

Companies that are looking for inquisitive, creative, engaged, and motivated coworkers cannot deny the creativity and performance potential of women. Many women in Germany have had an excellent education, yet in most businesses and public institutions they are still fighting for recognition, especially when it comes to filling leadership positions.[97] At the same time, 66.8 percent of all women are employed, and 49.7 percent of students are women. Women are ahead of men in scores on their high school exams and in achieving degrees, including in the natural sciences. In comparison, the percentage of women who are moving up to the executive level is only 10 percent—a shockingly low number.

Most male executives today are married and have a family, while women in leadership positions often pay for their dedication by remaining childless. Over 40 percent of women academics between the ages of thirty-five and forty do not have children. The expectations of executives are immense, in terms of professional dedication and the commitment of time and strength. Time for one's personal life quickly diminishes, including time for one's family. Women are just as much affected as men are, with the difference that it is usually women who are also responsible for the family, and who are quicker to relinquish having a family when in leadership positions.

Conversely, many highly qualified women refrain from taking on positions of responsibility because they are afraid they won't be able to align their desire for a family with their professional career. But the latest studies show that desire for a family is not what keeps a woman from having a career, as has been thought. Rather, 47 percent of those surveyed felt that it was prejudice against women that restrained their career potential. And 34 percent of women counted the lack of professional networks as a major stumbling block for the advancement of their career.

Our society is losing out on enormous potential. A woman's good education is much too valuable to simply be abandoned. Studies have long indicated that so-called mixed leadership is in many cases more successful than if men alone are at the helm. Modern brain research has once and for all laid to rest the preconception that male intelligence is superior to female intelligence. It has, however, discovered extraordinary differences between the thinking of men and women.[98]

Men and women differ not in the level of their intelligence but in their type of intelligence. While male and female brains are the same, they work in different ways. Men and women organize their thoughts differently, and they develop alternate solutions for the same circumstances. Hormones also shape the male and female intellect differently, affecting the microstructure of the brain even in utero. As newborns, boys and girls already perceive the world in different ways. Besides the genetic legacy, our environment also has a lasting effect on the differences between men and women. Even if both sexes are intellectually equal, they distinguish themselves greatly in terms of the specific cognitive output in the same circumstances. A man and a woman with an equal level of intelligence can come up with completely different solutions when solving the same problem. However, both men and women can be equally unwilling to consider the other's perspective when arriving at their own conclusion. Not acknowledging the other's point of view is the source of many misunderstandings. But therein also lies a hidden, untapped potential. Because if women see something that men cannot, and vice versa, then the combination of the two points of view can help avoid simplistic and one-sided answers to complex problems and can lead to powerful solutions. It has been proven that women are more quickly able to grasp nonverbal connections. Women's perception is more complex. The old adage that a women on a team will bring complications may be true, but in a positive way. Women rely more strongly on their intuitive and memory-based awareness, which leads to a more complex and creative perspective. When a female brain evaluates a situation, it looks for similarities among the broad range of past experiences. In this way women have been proven to be superior to men in terms of quickly assessing a situation, being sensitive to emotional states, and perceiving differences in facts.

The two genders use their brains differently. Women use the evolutionarily younger areas of the brain, where they can interpret facial expressions, gestures, and other methods of communication, more frequently than men do. Men, on the other hand, are always connected to the more ancient parts of the brain, even when they are at rest. This part of the brain is wired for survival—it's as if a man has to be ready to fight at any moment.

These differences in the workings of the intellect lead men to frequently seek out very even-keeled solutions. Women, on the other hand, often want to examine all the details step by step, which can sometimes get in the way of quick results. Scientists describe these two attitudes as "high-risk gambler" and "safe investor."

I have had many exchanges with women in government and economics about this issue. I was especially impressed by Lore Maria Peschel-Gutzeit, Berlin's former minister of justice.[99] During her long career as a politician and as a justice, this mother of three was involved in establishing legal equality for women in Germany. Today Peschel-Gutzeit is pursuing the stronger integration of women onto executive and supervisory boards. Her reasoning is that men ask questions less often, while women will seek detailed information, thus taking on a monitoring function on a board. Since the economic crisis has brought to light the failure of control mechanisms, she is especially advocating more women at the executive level.

I, too, am convinced that having women in leadership positions could advance our companies' creativity and our future sustainability, especially because men and women employ such different strategies. We need concrete action from economics, politics, business, and various alliances in order to right this societal wrong. Only when the two sexes are working together can all the decision makers of our society reach their full potential. We need to realize that women's complex perception can complement the tunnel vision that men can sometimes develop. Conversely, men can remain focused on a goal even within the most multitiered problems, which is a very complementary quality for women to work with.

In today's world, where the challenges could not be any more complex, a great potential lies in these differences. Businesses that bank on women in leadership positions have an advantage in market competition. Female managers are important to the success of communications strategies and creativity—and for the future of our society.

In the United States, training specifically geared toward female executives has long been the norm. In Germany, Bertelsmann has set a first such benchmark by offering an executive development seminar every year at our Business Women School in Berlin, in which twenty-four women from various German businesses participate.[100] Renowned women speakers who are active in economics, the media, religion, and politics give insight into their professional experience. I greatly enjoy using this opportunity to speak with some of our young participants. It is quite impressive how highly motivated these women are as they search for the right strategy for their career path.

Together we look at how women's competence, their knowledge, and their capabilities can be integrated into the corporate culture. We openly discuss questions about leadership competence and career issues. The reconciliation of work and family life is an important subject for many. Having successful speakers as role models in an open working atmosphere makes the Business Women School a place that's full of opportunity. The young managers of tomorrow have the chance here to network and compare experiences. Everyone takes full advantage of these opportunities.

A future-oriented society cannot be built without

collaboration between men and women. Many young women still underestimate, however, how much effort it takes, even after a successful career start, to get a foot through the door on the leadership level. This is why I appeal to women to take on responsibility not just for others but for themselves as well. We need more than a commitment on the parts of corporations—we also have to change the thinking in our own heads.

Migration and Integration as Challenges

My friend Yue-Sai Kan, a businesswoman and an author well known in China and in Western countries,[101] once said to me, "You Europeans aren't curious enough." This statement got me thinking. What is it that so often immobilizes us Europeans, or makes us think that we know everything better? Why do we feel superior to people from other cultures? Is this just a lack of curiosity? Or is it the arrogance that is part of traditional Western culture that makes us act this way, that leaves us easily satisfied and closes the door to new insights?

Many times my curiosity about other people has tested the patience of my companions. Not everyone shares my enthusiasm for things foreign. Encounters and experiences with other cultures can be exhausting, but they are always enriching. They expand our horizons and teach us to look at life through new eyes. Having encountered a variety of perspectives is a great opportunity, one that can be discovered only by traveling in other countries and on other continents. We must grab at these opportunities with our bare hands—they are part of our lives.

But we have to be open and aware to take advantage of them.[102]

In the past decades, German society has fundamentally changed demographically. The integration of immigrants is no longer merely an issue about minorities. The sustainability of our aging society is largely dependent on whether we are able to successfully integrate people from different origins, with diverse cultural backgrounds, and with different social statuses.

Today approximately 20 percent of people living in Germany have an immigrant background. The varying birthrates among different population groups will drive this number up. We thus need to see change as an opportunity and accept different points of view. In the coming years, Germany will be extremely dependent on immigration. Unfortunately, going through a financial crisis makes the growth of new attitudes more difficult. The challenge to our society is to support the peaceful coexistence of people from different backgrounds, despite any existing social tensions. To me personally, this is an important issue that I continually pursue in my many conversations and discussions.

The Bertelsmann Foundation has developed its own focus on integration and offers a number of projects, studies, and measures to support a successful integration policy.[103] The future of our democracy depends on the real-life implementation of values that connect our society, like tolerance, a sense of community, and civic engagement. To implement them, appropriate models must be developed. Together with our partners, we have created educational programs that support the corresponding personal attitudes. Germany's many years of treating immigration as a taboo topic have sadly paved the way for an attitude of hostility toward foreigners. We must fight this with all our might.

This problem is now part of our politics. Integration has become a key element in determining the future of our society. But there is still much to do, and many changes to be made. A doctor from Bulgaria should not have to work here as a nurse, and an engineer from Kenya must not have to drive a taxi to make ends meet. A survey by the Bertelsmann Foundation on democracy and integration in Germany[104] demonstrated that a great majority of immigrants are supporters of democracy: 70 percent of all immigrants surveyed thought democracy is the best form of government. A true commitment to Germany is also reflected in the fact that 83 percent of those who are immigrants feel connected to this country.

German society has to meet this commitment. A successful integration of immigrants is a major contributor to social cohesion. This includes having equal access to education. But studies show that in Germany, unlike in most other countries, educational success is hugely dependent on one's origin.

About a year ago I happened upon the following scene. It was the end of August, and the new school year had just begun. A father and his young daughter were approaching a school that I was scheduled to visit that morning. The little girl was dressed especially nicely—she had bows in her hair and was wearing a pretty summer dress. Full of pride, she carried a *Schultüte,* a large cone full of sweets, a tradition in Germany for the first day of school. You could see the intense anticipation on the faces of both father and daughter. They were both from Sri Lanka, I later found out.

I was speaking with a teacher, who turned to the two with great surprise. The first day of school was not until the next day—the father had not correctly read the registration form. I will never forget the disappointment on their faces. What an unlucky beginning!

This experience is an example of the bureaucratic and human hurdles that still stand in the way of full participation in our society. Before we can successfully integrate everyone through education, we must counsel parents and take small and large steps, like giving systematic language support, cultivating openness, and offering advisory support for those in the children's surroundings.

Part of our foundation's core identity is that we all feel called upon to recognize social problems and to look beyond our own four walls—that is, to look around the world—to find the best solutions.

With the Reinhard Mohn Prize, the Bertelsmann Foundation gives backing to innovative concepts and exemplary solutions for societal challenges.[105] In 2008 we were particularly looking at models for successful integration through education and tried to see where and how children from immigrant families can have equal education opportunities. Our commission spoke with more than one hundred education experts in ten classic immigrant countries, from Canada to England, Sweden, and Switzerland.

We were especially impressed by the regional school board of Toronto, which had developed a persuasive strategy to encourage school participation of all children and young people, no matter what their background.[106] More than 550 schools are part of the Toronto District school boards. They all share the core principles of equal opportunity and participation. This gives everyone, from principals to students, the responsibility to stand up for fairness and integration. Toronto is the only school board in Canada that has created a leadership position for this responsibility. Diversity is supported and valued in all schools, and the school board assists the teachers to receive the necessary qualifications. The school culture in Toronto is a big proponent of candor toward a child's environment—for example, by giving parents access to counselors who can help with integration. Schools that are situated in especially troubled neighborhoods receive support through additional initiatives. Besides methodical and continuous language study, the schools investigate the different origins of the students, both within the curriculum and in daily life. This way every student is made to feel welcome with his own life story and his family's background.

This brief overview makes it clear how far we still have to go if we want to succeed at integration. Step by step, we should look at the following goals:

Diversity in society should no longer be viewed as a problem, but rather as an opportunity.

Our school system needs a new model for the equal participation of all children and young people, no matter what their background.

Our learning culture must develop models for granting individual aid.

Continuous teacher education is a must.

We must strengthen the regional support system: Who is more familiar with local challenges than the local community?

Schools need the assistance of committed outside partners to implement their integration strategies.

If all these steps are put into place, successful social integration will no longer be a dream. Every child in our country should have a chance to make something of their life. It is the duty of our society to support and encourage these children. The right way to do this is still up for discussion. There is no question for me, however, that children must be at the center of the debate—because children are our future!

Building Bridges for the Future

"You always saw the world as your workplace," my husband said to me during the last summer we spent together, in 2009. He smiled while he said it, and I thought about our many trips—and the numerous initiatives that grew out of them both for Bertelsmann AG and for the Bertelsmann Foundation. My husband, who loved peace and quiet and who preferred to return to his private life after a hard week of working, had a wife at his side who loved nothing more than being among people.

Encounters with people inspire me, whether they are cashiers at a supermarket, or scientists, or well-known personalities, or the coworkers of our company. I always get new energy from my interactions with others. My observations often lead to new impulses, new ideas, new initiatives and projects.

Every human being has their own personality, interests, and ideas. You have to have a feel for these interests, for they open the doors to conversation, to shared initiatives, and sometimes even to year-long undertakings.

Even as a young girl, I always openly approached

people. Later, at my husband's side, I valued this openness. If I want to get to know somebody, I have no fear of an encounter. For me, the person is always at the center—nothing else matters. I also never let a language barrier stop me, because a person's eyes, gestures, and posture tell me so very much about him or her that it never matters whether we are in Asia, Africa, the United States, or Europe.

In the 1980s, it become clear that globalization was going to change our world. Economic and geopolitical shifts have created immense changes. People's wish for peace and prosperity is all that has remained the same. Countries and businesses cannot close the door on globalization. No matter where in this world we live and work, we depend on the opportunities of international trade relations. Yet we live in neither a European, nor an American, nor an Asian century: our century can only be lived globally! Globalization is rapidly expanding, and our international interdependence in economics, technology, and politics cannot be undone. Whatever happens today in New York, the whole world quickly knows, and any events in Japan or in the Middle East will reach us shortly.

In recent years, countless numbers of people have become integrated into the global labor market. Never before have there been so many growth opportunities for people all over the world. But there has also never been such a big risk of being affected by a problem or a crisis that is happening anywhere. The financial crisis of 2008 and 2009 clearly demonstrated this. The sudden standstill of European flights because of the eruption of a volcano in Iceland had repercussions for all of us. Everybody is connected with everybody else. But are we as humans really aware of the incredible responsibility that arises from this connection? Are we equipped to face these challenges? Isn't our world still a patchwork of conflicting interests, deceptive maneuvering, tedious compromises, and fragile alliances that could all fall apart at any moment?

Countless wars and conflicts envelop the globe. What really gives us hope among these conflicting interests? What gives us meaning? What gives us the courage, day after day, to tackle new responsibilities? And what keeps us from despair?

My own optimism can reach its limits. Many conversations lead nowhere, and I know the frustration of repeated efforts without success. When there is bad news, I feel desperate, and I get fearful and worried. Yet every failure is offset by a success, and every disappointment is followed by a glimmer of hope. At times like this, I'm reminded of what my teacher used to tell me: "Try it. You can do it." And if one thing doesn't work, another will.

Every day is a bridge into the future that I want to cross. I was very lucky to be able to have had the experience of creating something. This opportunity is also an obligation, one that I have day after day, and year after year. I am deeply convinced that you must try the impossible in order to achieve the possible. It can be very tiring for those around me. My coworkers know a thing or two about me not giving up, even after ten tries. But once we've reached our goal, we are all happy together again. All the hard work is forgotten once an initiative has succeeded or when an idea leads to a wonderful success.

We all have to make our own contributions to our future; it is no longer possible to simply take refuge behind our country's government. Every positive encounter with a person from another background is another building block for our shared future. Over the years I have met many notable personalities who share my burning interest in a successful dialogue that reaches across countries, continents, origins, and languages. I love bringing people together and keeping my eyes and ears open for perspectives that can connect people across all borders. My curiosity and my burning desire to learn, which I always had with me when I first accompanied my husband on our international travels, is still a part of who I am today.

Borne by the experience of our shared lives, I want to carry into the future the conviction that the development of a global conscience is our cultural responsibility.

The cultural diversity with which we are surrounded is a treasure that we need to preserve. At the same time, it is absolutely necessary that we build bridges of communication through cultural exchanges, because cultural factors still play a big role in the creation of worldwide conflicts.

In conjunction with the Heidelberg University Institute of Conflict Research, Bertelsmann undertook an empirical study that examined all the conflicts that have been recorded around the world since 1945 and quantified their causes and intensity.[107] The study showed a big jump in political conflicts, although in four out of five cases, these conflicts occurred within national borders.

Our study did not, however, deliver any evidence for Samuel Huntington's theory of the "clash of civilizations,"[108] like that of the West with Islam, which is supported by many other prominent scientists. As soon as culture plays a role in major global conflicts, these conflicts are especially prone to erupt in violence. Particularly notable in intrastate conflicts is the interplay between memberships in different language groups and the presence of an excessive number of young men between fifteen and twenty-four years old.

Our study showed that cultural factors can often heighten existing conflicts but are not usually the cause of conflict. The support of cultural exchanges and of communication between cultures can have a tremendous stabilizing power. Cultural exchange is peacekeeping.

During these times of rapidly expanding global development, building cultural bridges is a must.

An important forum for these efforts is the Salzburger Trilogue,[109] of which we have been a supporter since 2001. This initiative grew out of our experiences in our international cultural forum series. The former Austrian chancellor Wolfgang Schüssel and I led this initiative to assemble the most interesting cultural, economic, and political personalities for a vibrant and dedicated exchange of ideas. Every year scientists, influential decision makers, and shapers of opinion from all the continents are invited by the Bertelsmann Foundation and the Austrian Foreign Ministry for a gathering in Salzburg. Here the most pressing political challenges can be openly and publicly discussed without the constraint of national responsibilities or political partiality.

In 2009, the focus of the Salzburg Trilogue was the theme "World Crises and Human Potential."[110] Moderated by Wolfgang Schüssel, the discussion evolved around the global symptoms of crises in our time, as well as possible tactics for sustainable development. But not just established and experienced speakers were heard here. We also invited young experts and new entrepreneurs to take part in this high-caliber debate. Many of them took advantage of the opportunity. The initiation and growth of new networks here, along with the public work that follows, is a special passion of mine. I am convinced that exactly these types of initiatives and networks will deliver desperately needed new impulses to our political decision makers and government institutions.

Our global era is facing numerous unresolved challenges. Martin Lees, the former secretary general of the Club of Rome, of which I have been a member for many years, clearly stated in Salzburg what is our most important task at hand: to look at problems not in isolation, but to recognize how greatly all our problems—as well as our actions—are interconnected.

The American futurist Jerome Glenn, who founded the Millennium Project,[111] analyzed fifteen global challenges, whose reciprocal effects on one another can help us estimate the future of mankind. But which of today's crises deserve our greatest attention?

One is certainly global warming—the global climate change that could threaten the existence of man. It will make entire land tracts uninhabitable, which will lead to extensive population migration, which will then have an impact on countries even if they were not directly impacted. The failure of the international climate change conference in Copenhagen in 2009 demonstrated how difficult it is to arrive at an international consensus on actions that urgently need to be taken on this issue.

The second big problem area is the disparity between the rich industrial countries and those countries in which poverty, indifference, poor health conditions, and social injustice dominate. Alexander Likhotal, the president of Green Cross International, sees worldwide poverty as the mother of all problems that we are facing today. He states that basically 50 percent of the world's population receives absolutely no advantages from globalization. If we consider that in fifty years almost 9.2 billion people will be living on the earth, most of them in developing countries, we get a sense of what kind of challenges we will be facing. Many people do not have access to health care or education. But without education, a self-determined life, positive economic development, and political participation in society are not possible. No wonder 60 percent of people around the world view globalization with fear and uncertainty. The belief in the advantages of globalization is fading. The most recent financial crises have made it clear that we must pay closer attention than ever before to the risks involved in globalization.

Europe and the European Union are standing at a crossroads. We all must ask ourselves, What does the future that we imagine look like? Globalization must not degenerate into a massive game, in which a few winners stand facing millions of losers. The Indian sociologist Surendra Munshi has illustrated that without an underlying ethic of responsible political action and a consensus of humanistic values, we will most likely not be able to overcome the challenges of globalization.[112]

Other problem areas are rapid population growth, human rights, ecological resources, energy sources, and security. The following example shows how closely these problem areas are interconnected. If the water supply on earth should diminish in the next decades, conflicts over distribution will increase, and poverty around the world will grow.

The global connection of these enormous problem areas and of sociopolitical challenges places new demands on the political decision makers. The problem areas of the future are much more existential in nature than they've been before. During earlier wars and conflicts, there were always areas and resources in the world where people could flee, places they could make their own. This time we're all in the same boat, and there is no way out.

If democracy is to survive as a governing principle, political leadership can no longer operate solely within the cycle of elections. The challenges of our times call for political leadership that looks beyond its immediate interests to the long term. We also have to make people in our society open to these developments in order for there to be any progress. Political and economic leaders are called upon to look beyond the here and now, and to see into the future. The future cannot be claimed by just one nation or one continent. The future concerns us all.

Again and again, the conversations I have everywhere

on the globe circle back to the question of whether decision makers will be able to successfully communicate to the public the mutual responsibility we have for our planet, and whether they will be able to make this agenda acceptable to the political majority. If we want to give peace a chance worldwide, the perspectives and hopes of all people must be heard.

No government or political system will be able to solve all the problems that come with globalization on its own.[113] Many institutions these days have been stretched to the limit. This is why everyone is called upon to think beyond their nation, their culture, and their political, economic, and scientific interests. After a decades-long climate of confrontation among different interest groups, the time has come to create a climate of cooperation and shared responsibility. We don't need just new institutions for the twenty-first century; we need to create informal groups and networks. In our global world, no state or institution will be able to achieve an organized balance of interests on its own. In heretofore unknown ways, political decision makers will have to continuously look for allies if they want to realize their goals.

We can meet the challenges of globalization only if we are willing to share them. Our willingness to share our prosperity is an important key to achieving peace. Just engaging with other cultures' and nations' interests opens our eyes to new ways of developing our economic systems. Without an ecological balance and a culture of sustainability, there will be no long-term quality of life, without which a social market economy cannot survive.

Just a few years ago many in Germany believed that our country's growth, prosperity, and job opportunities would go on indefinitely. The rapid technical innovations led many to believe that there was a solution for everything. Confidence turned into carelessness, and optimism grew into irresponsibility. Despite our economic successes, many developments of that time carried within them the seeds for today's circumstances. Since then many businesses have been caught in a dangerous global downward spiral. As a result, millions of people now fear for their livelihood. The great opportunities of globalization that came into being with the worldwide technological interconnection and the ever faster exchange of economic, cultural, and political content have now shown us their dark side. We must seriously ask ourselves what effects this crisis will have on our democracy, our social system, the social market economy, and the labor market.

All the leading politicians of the last few years closed their eyes to the crisis happening in the European Union. In a most unwarrantable way, citizens were denied a clear understanding of the facts. All the economic specialists had long been aware that Greece was excessively indebted, and that Spain, Italy, Ireland, and Portugal were the next candidates for a debt crisis. For me, the social unrest that is taking place in Greece and France is the precursor to serious social conflicts. If such unrest continues, it could pose a significant threat to the European Community, which was put together with such great dedication.

When I watch the daily news, like so many other people, I feel despair. But then I think about the little girl from Wiedenbrück, born into a world that seemed so hopeless. How much has happened since then! How much has been achieved in our country!

We as Germans can be proud of our country. Together we rebuilt after World War II and were able to achieve peace and prosperity. The peaceful reunification of the two German states is an especially successful chapter in our history. This success, however, is also an obligation to take responsibility for the whole of society.

With its social market economy, Germany has been better able to weather the economic crisis than many other countries. Over many decades, the social market economy has proven to be an economically stabilizing force and has established the conditions for social unity. It is up to us to pass along this experience, and to champion a humane process of globalization in our dialogue with other cultures and nations. There surely won't be a lack of conflicts, but every crisis is also an opportunity to further develop existing systems and institutions. In my life I have often discovered that change opens new windows—windows that give us the opportunity to think critically about our actions. We suddenly recognize opportunities that we never even noticed before. We should use this chance.

A number of developments should encourage us. I personally hope very much that especially young people will take advantage of the opportunity to gain information and new experiences from the Internet that take them beyond their own cultures. People from all over the planet can exchange ideas and learn from one another in ways never before possible. What a fantastic opportunity to share the ideals of tolerance, prudence, solidarity, and civility.

"Looking over the fence" leads to new perspectives for solutions and plans of action. Our world needs to be in an interdisciplinary, partner-based dialogue to ensure future growth, and the employment and prosperity that result from this growth. We must redefine our efforts for sustainability and in this way gain confidence in shared values, which are indispensable to our efforts.

Again and again in my encounters, I experience hope, faith, optimism, and especially dynamic activity. No—giving up just isn't for me. I firmly believe that every one of us can contribute their part to the success of the future.

Liz Mohn Honors

Bambi Media Award
As part of the Bambi awards ceremony on October 27, 1996, in Leipzig, Liz Mohn was honored in the Charity category for her dedication to the German Stroke Aid Foundation.

Great Cross of Merit
In 2000, Liz Mohn received the Great Cross of Merit of the Federal Republic of Germany.

Honorary Membership in the Círculo de Confianza
On October 25, 2006, Liz Mohn was made an honorary member of the Círculo de Confianza in Spain. High-ranking representatives of the Spanish economic and banking sectors, including the chair, Francisco Belil (who is also president of the German Chamber of Commerce for Spain), thereby honored Liz Mohn for her years of dedication on behalf of Spain and for improving Spanish-German relations.

Order of Merit of North Rhine–Westphalia

On December 12, 2006, Liz Mohn received North Rhine–Westphalia's Order of Merit. In his congratulatory speech, Jürgen Rüttgers, the premier of North Rhine–Westphalia, emphasized Liz Mohn's commitment to peaceful coexistence in future generations.

Vernon A. Walters Award

On June 13, 2008, in New York, Liz Mohn received the Vernon A. Walters Award. She was honored for her commitment to promoting transatlantic relations and her engagement in German-Jewish relations. In his laudation, Kofi Annan praised Liz Mohn's engagement as a "builder of bridges" between people of different origins, ethnicities, and religions.

The UNESCO Children in Need Award

At the UNESCO gala on November 1, 2008, in Cologne, Liz Mohn received the Children in Need Award for her long and extraordinary social engagement as president of the German Stroke Aid Foundation.

Karl Winnacker Prize

On August 21, 2009, in Marburg, Liz Mohn became the first woman to receive the Karl Winnacker Prize. It is handed out every two years by the Marburg University

Association for commendable support for the collaboration of universities and industry in the natural sciences.

Global Economy Prize

On June 20, 2010, Liz Mohn received the prestigious Global Economy Prize, along with Pascal Lamy, the director general of the World Trade Organization, and Paul Krugman, Nobel laureate in economics. Every year the Kiel Institute for the World Economy awards the prize to one economist, one politician, and one businessperson, who stand out as pioneers for an open market economy and are especially focused on social justice.

Notes

1. Antonio R. Damasio, *The Feeling of What Happens: Body and Emotion in the Making of Consciousness* (Boston, 2000); Gerd Gigerenzer, *Gut Feelings: The Intelligence of the Unconscious* (New York, 2007); Daniel Goleman, *Emotional Intelligence* (New York, 1995); Gerald Hüther, *Bedienungsanleitung für ein Menschliches Gehirn* (Instructions for the Human Brain) (Göttingen, 2009); Ernst Pöppel, *Zum Entscheiden Geboren. Hirnforschung für Manager* (Born to Decide: Brain Research for Managers) (Munich, 2008); Gerhard Roth, *Fühlen, Denken, Handeln. Wie das Gehirn unser Verhalten steuert* (Feeling, Thinking, Doing: How the Brain Steers Our Behavior) (Frankfurt, 2003); Maja Storch, *Das Geheimnis kluger Entscheidungen. Von somatischen Markern, Bauchgefühl und Überzeugungskraft* (The Secret of Intelligent Decisions: Somatic Markers, Gut Feelings, and the Power of Persuasion) (Munich, 2005).

2. These early initiatives are documented in the archives of the Bertelsmann Foundation, Collection ABSt, AS0051.

3. Ibid. Liz Mohn has been on the advisory board of the Bertelsmann Foundation since 1986. She began to lead the Health Care topic area in 1982, and starting in 1992 she led the foundation's Culture topic area. In 2000 she joined the executive board. Since January 2005 she has been vice chair of the executive board.

4. Reinhard Mohn, *Success Through Partnership: An Entrepreneurial Strategy* (New York, 1988); Reinhard Mohn, *Humanity Wins: A Strategy for Progress and Leadership in Times of Change* (New York, 2000); Reinhard Mohn, *An Age of New Possibilities: How Humane Values and an Entrepreneurial Spirit Will Lead Us into the Future* (New York, 2004); Reinhard Mohn, *Von der Welt lernen. Erfolg durch Menschlichkeit und Freiheit* (Learning from the World: Success Through Humanity and Freedom) (Munich, 2008).

5. Carol Dweck, *The New Psychology of Success* (New York, 2008); Howard Gardner, *Five Minds for the Future* (Cambridge, 2007); Richard Layard, *Happiness from a New Science* (New York, 2005); Nassim Nicholas Taleb, *The Black Swan: The Impact of the Highly Improbable* (New York, 2007).

6. Archives of the Bertelsmann Foundation, Collection ABSt, AS0051.

7. Ibid., *Report of the Bertelsmann Foundation: 4th Quarter 1981–1st Quarter 1988*.

8. *First Annual Report of the Bertelsmann Foundation* (Gütersloh, 1982), p. 23.

9. *Third Annual Report of the Bertelsmann Foundation 1985–1986* (Gütersloh, 1987), pp. 29–30. The title of the conference was "The Future of Publishing Across Language Frontiers." On this trip, Reinhard Mohn was given the honor of "Friend of the City of Jerusalem" through Teddy Kollek.

10. *Third Annual Report of the Bertelsmann Foundation*, pp. 102–103; *Westfalen-Blatt*, Sept. 25, 1986; *Allgemeine Jüdische Wochenzeitung*, Dec. 14, 1986.

11. For project length, see *Business Report 1987–1989, Business Report 1990*, pp. 57–58.

12. Kai Bosecker, ed., *Projekte der Bertelsmann Stiftung mit Bezug auf Israel* (Projects of the Bertelsmann Foundation

Regarding Israel), Jul. 17, 2008, p. 4; see also "Kollek, Teddy: Ein neuer Deutsche wie er im Buche Steht" (Kollek, Teddy: A New German by the Book), in Thomas Middlehof, Gerd Schulte-Hillen, and Gunter Thielen, eds., *Reinhard Mohn. Unternehemer–Stifter–Bürger* (Reinhard Mohn: Entrepreneur, Philanthropist, Citizen) (Gütersloh, 2001), pp. 93–96.

13. *Annual Report of the Bertelsmann Foundation 1992*, pp. 55–56; *Annual Report of the Bertelsmann Foundation 1995–96*, pp. 68–69.

14. *Annual Report of the Bertelsmann Foundation 1993*, pp. 56–57.

15. Boseker, *Projekte mit Bezug auf Israel*, pp. 3–4.

16. Stephan Vopel, in *Einblick. Das Mitarbeitermagazin der Bertelsmann Stiftung* (Insight: The Magazine for the Co-workers of the Bertelsmann Foundation) (June 2000), p. 7.

17. Introduction and Chronology of the project Kulturraum Europa—Zwischen Einheit und Vielfalt. Strategie and Optionen für die Zukunft Europas (Culture in Europe—Between Unity and diversity. Strategies and Options for the Future of Europe), compiled by Kai Franke, from *Chronik der Bertelsmann Stiftung—von 1977 bis heute* (Chronicle of the Bertelsmann Foundation—from 1977 Until Today) (Gütersloh, 2011).

18. Ibid.

19. Ibid.

20. On March 21, 1995, in Giza, near Cairo, Egypt's first public library was opened: the Giza Public Library. In planning it, Bertelsmann was able draw on its experience building the city library of Gütersloh, as well as the model library Can Torró in Spain. This knowledge was transposed to the realm of Arabic culture. The project continued with the opening of a branch library in the Cairo neighborhood Zaytoun. The library program is part of the educational initiative of

the Egyptian government. In 1998 Egypt received the annual UNESCO award for the fight against illiteracy.

21. In 1977 Dr. Gerd Wixforth, a city councilor of Gütersloh, and Reinhard Mohn, the chair of Bertelsmann AG, developed the idea of building a new, exemplary library for Gütersloh. In March experts gathered for an open hearing to discuss how a modern library should be equipped. Representatives of the Bertelsmann Foundation and of the city of Gütersloh visited libraries in Scandinavia. The insights and experiences they gleaned were integrated into the project. On May 4, 1984, the City Library of Gütersloh, LLC, had its official opening. Since then, with the support of the Bertelsmann Foundation, it has actively helped shape and innovate library developments internationally.

22. Samuel Huntington, *The Clash of Civilizations* (New York, 1996).

23. With its German-Egyptian Cultural Forum, which took place on February 21, 2001, in Cairo, the Bertelsmann Foundation began a New Dialogue series on an international level. The forum was an opportunity for both countries to exchange their experiences of globalization and its resulting effects. See Liz Mohn, *A Cultural Forum: Promoting Cultural Identity in the Age of Globalization: A German-Egyptian Experience* (Gütersloh, 2002).

24. The goal of the project, which continued until December 2009, was to advance intercultural communication on all levels, in order to promote long-lasting corporate success around the world. The project was divided into the following areas of responsibility: corporate governance, intercompany cooperation, Chinese companies in Germany, and diversity management.

25. L. Mohn, *Cultural Forum.*

26. Liz Mohn, ed., *Corporate Cultures in Global Interaction: Global Business Culture—An International Workshop Held in November 2002 in Gütersloh* (Gütersloh, 2003).

27. For the results of this exchange, see Bertelsmann Foundation, ed., *Asia Changes the World* (Gütersloh, 2007).

28. Liz Mohn, ed., *Cultures in Globalization: A Europe-India Dialogue on Global Challenges and Cultural Visions* (Gütersloh, 2006). In November 2005, the International Cultural Forum of New Delhi brought together Indian and European decision makers to spotlight the effects of globalization on culture and to reflect on means of communication. The hosts of this cooperative undertaking were Liz Mohn and Venkatraman Krishnamurthy, a representative of the Rajiv Gandhi Foundation.

29. During his first international trip after the dissolution of the Soviet Union, the former head of state Mikhail Gorbachev visited the Bertelsmann Foundation in Gütersloh. As president of the foundation that he established and that was named after him, he met with the boards of German foundations to discuss the possibilities for cooperation and support. See Archive of the Bertelsmann Foundation, Chronicle 1992.

30. Hans Meinke, "Per aspera ad astra—40 Jahre Unternehmer und Stifter in Spanien" (40 Years Entrepreneur and Benefactor in Spain), in Middlehof, Schulte-Hillen, and Thielen, *Reinhard Mohn*, pp. 233–42.

31. In 1995 Reinhard Mohn founded the Fundación Bertelsmann, based in Barcelona, to support the Spanish media and book culture, aid public libraries in Spain, and help with continuing education for the leadership staff. The Fundación Bertelsmann uses proven models for public library reform in Germany as its reference—for example, the city library in Gütersloh. The Bertelsmann Foundation's involvement in Spain

began in 1989 with the founding of the model library Can Torró in Alcúdia on Majorca. To provide for construction, on December 29, 1988, the city of Alcúdia and the Bertelsmann Foundation founded the Fundacíon Biblioteca de Alcúdia. The library's main focus was to promote literacy among children and youth through the close collaboration with schools. This project was successfully completed, and management of the library was handed over to the city of Alcúdia. With its library program, the Fundación Bertelsmann aims to establish new administrative methods in public libraries, promote reading among the population, provide access to information, and ensure the continuing education of librarians.

32. The Fundación Bertelsmann was founded in 1995 in Barcelona by Reinhard Mohn. The Spanish foundation shares with the Bertelsmann Foundation core values like freedom, solidarity, competence, and humanity, which guide the foundation's pursuit of future-oriented and sustainable social solutions. The Fundación Bertelsmann has the following goals: (1) to support social change in Spain; (2) to prepare society for the future; and (3) to promote social responsibility. In its first ten years of existence, the Fundación Bertelsmann mostly focused on the library system, including projects to support literacy and library improvement. In 2005, the foundation, under the chairmanship of Liz Mohn, decided to redirect its strategy. It now initiates projects geared toward the development of civic society, under the overarching theme of "social responsibility."

33. R. Mohn, *Von der Welt lernen,* pp. 30ff.

34. The Bertelsmann Foundation North America, founded in 2008, is based in Washington and represents the Bertelsmann Foundation in the United States. It encourages social change, advocates freedom of the individual and of societies,

and promotes international communication. The Bertelsmann Foundation acts as a bridge between Europe and America by sharing best practices on both sides of the Atlantic in foreign policy, economics, and social policy, on the premise that sooner or later both sides will be facing the same challenges, and that Europeans and Americans can learn from each other's solutions.

35. Henry Kissinger, "Transatlantische Partnerschaft oder europäischer Sonderweg?" (Transatlantic Partnership or Europe's Own Path?), in Middlehof, Schulte-Hillen, and Thielen, *Reinhard Mohn,* pp. 45–51.

36. Liz Mohn, acceptance speech for the Walters Award, New York, June 13, 2008.

37. *Annual Reports of the Bertelsmann Foundation 1984–1992.*

38. *Annual Reports of the Bertelsmann Foundation 1989–2001.* According to the bylaws of the German Uveitis Association, its purpose was to support "research on intraocular inflammation (uveitis) and associated illnesses, as well as the dissemination of information and the education of patients and doctors nationally and internationally." It also supported uveitis self-help groups. Research projects were undertaken at several universities. The German Uveitis Association was dissolved on December 31, 2001.

39. *Annual Report of the Bertelsmann Foundation on the Neurology Projects I, II, III, in 1984–1992.*

40. Ibid., ABST, AS0051/69.

41. *Auditor's Report 1994,* German Stroke Aid Foundation, p. 2.

42. For current activities of the German Stroke Aid Foundation, see *Annual Report of the Stroke Aid Foundation 2008* and www.schlaganfall-hilfe.de.

43. According to *Annual Report of the Bertelsmann Foundation*, preventive care health exams were taken by coworkers at Hoechst, BMW, Deutsche Bank, and Bertelsmann, among others in 1996–97.

44. *Annual Reports of the Bertelsmann Foundation 1992–94.* See *Auditor's Report 1994* of the Academy of Manual Medicine.

45. On the project's progress, see *Annual Reports of the Bertelsmann Foundation 1990–99*; and Bertelsmann Foundation, ed., *Mineralstoffe, Spurenelemente und Vitamine in der Gesundheitsvorsorge. Was Sie darüber wissen sollten* (Minerals, Trace Elements and Vitamins in Health Care: What You Should Know) (Gütersloh, 1998).

46. See "Gesundheit," at www.bertelsmann-Stiftung.de/Gesundheit.

47. The member businesses of the European network Enterprise for Health worked to develop a partnership-based corporate culture and an exemplary corporate health care policy based on that culture. The project time period is January 1, 2001–December 31, 2006. See also *Successful, Healthy Enterprises in Europe*, Brochure of the Bertelsmann Foundation, 2007.

48. At the end of October 2009, at the request of the Bertelsmann Foundation, TNS Emnid surveyed 1,003 German citizens. The survey is part of a foundation project that is examining the consequences of the economic crisis, and the prospects for Germany, until the year 2020.

49. *Erfolg durch Partnerschaft. Analyseergebnisse zum Zusammenhang zwischen Unternehmenskultur und wirtschaftlichem Erfolg* (Success Through Partnerships: Results of an Analysis of the Connection Between Corporate Culture and Financial Success) (Gütersloh, 2008).

50. *Vorgeschichte und Internationalisierung des Gesang-swettbewerbs "Neue Stimmen" 1987–1997* (Preliminary History and Internationalization of the Singing Contest "New Voices" 1987–1997), in Archives of the Bertelsmann Foundation. "Europäischer Sängerwettstreit erlebt ein glänzendes Debüt" (European Singing Competition Has a Glowing Debut) in *Neue Westfälische Zeitung*, Oct. 26, 1987. Until 1989 the contest was held every year. Since 1991 it has taken place every two years.

51. *Daten und Fakten zum internationalen Gesangswett-bewerb "Neue Stimmen" 1987–1999* (Dates and Facts on the International Singing Contest "New Voices"), compiled by Kai Bosecker, Sept. 10, 2008, in Archives of the Bertelsmann Foundation; see also *Change. Das Magazin der Bertelsmann Stiftung* (Change: The Magazine of the Bertelsmann Foundation), April 2009; and "Kultur," www.bertelsmann-Stiftung .de/Kultur.

52. See "Neue Stimmen: Internationaler Gesangswettbe-werb," at www.neue-stimmen.de.

53. In August 2009, at the request of the Bertelsmann Foundation, TNS Emnid surveyed 1,001 Germans of all age groups on the subject of classical music and opera.

54. To this day, communication and development through music is one of the foundation's priorities. We take our projects into preschools, elementary schools, and music academies to educate children musically and promote child development through music. The goals are to encourage creativity, to develop children's creative strengths, to champion the joy of music, to support physical and emotional well-being, to strengthen love of learning, and to improve schools' social environment. We try to make music accessible to all children.

55. See "Liz Mohn Kultur- und Musikstiftung," at www
.kultur-und-musikstiftung.de.

56. Daniel Barenboim, *A Life in Music* (New York, 2002).

57. R. Mohn, *Von der Welt lernen*, pp. 133ff.

58. Bertelsmann Foundation, ed., *Woran glaubt die Welt?
Analysen und Kommentare zum Religionsmonitor 2008*
(What Does the World Believe In? Analysis and Commentary
on the Religion Monitor 2008) (Gütersloh, 2009).

59. Ibid.

60. *175 Jahre Bertelsmann. Eine Zukunftsgeschichte* (175
Years of Bertelsmann: A Story for the Future) (Munich, 2010);
see also the preface by Hartmut Ostrowski, ibid., pp. 4ff. Bertelsmann is the oldest of the top ten media companies. After
Bertelsmann comes Vivendi (founded in 1853) and Cox Enterprises (founded in 1898).

61. R. Mohn, *Von der Welt lernen*, p. 17.

62. Ibid., pp. 30ff.

63. Bertelsmann Corporate Archive, Akz-Nr. 10/08.

64. R. Mohn, *Age of New Possibilities*; R. Mohn, *Von der
Welt lernen*.

65. Bertelsmann Essentials, at www.bertelsmann.com/
bertelsmann . . . /pdf_Essentials_Eng_0.pdf.

66. R. Mohn, *Von der Welt lernen*, pp. 99–100.

67. *The Rule of Benedict*, Chapter 3: "Do everything with
consultation and you will have no regrets when the deed is
done."

68. Damasio, *Feeling of What Happens;* Gigerenzer, *Gut
Feelings;* Goleman, *Emotional Intelligence;* Pöppel, *Zum Ent-
scheiden Geboren;* Roth, *Fühlen, Denken, Handeln;* Storch,
Das Geheimnis kluger Entscheidungen.

69. Storch, *Das Geheimnis kluger Entscheidungen.*

70. Gigerenzer, *Gut Feelings.*

71. Bertelsmann Essentials

72. See www.bertelsmann.com.

73. R. Mohn, *Von der Welt lernen.*

74. Liz Mohn, "On Corporate Culture," speech, in Bertelsmann AG Corporate Archive.

75. *Erfolg durch Partnershaft. Analyseergebnisse zum Zusammenhang zwischen Unternehmenskultur und wirtschaftlichem Erfolg* (Success Through Partnerships. Results of an Analysis of the Connection Between Corporate Culture and Financial Success) (Gütersloh, 2008).

76. On "Black Monday," October 27, 1987, the Dow Jones dropped by over 20 percent. This stock market crash led to a global economic crisis that reached Germany, if somewhat delayed, in 1991–92.

77. At the end of October 2009, at the request of the Bertelsmann Foundation, TNS Emnid surveyed 1,003 German citizens.

78. Because of its many insufficiently educated students, Germany is missing out on enormous potential growth—the cost will reach 2.8 trillion euros in the next eighty years, the average life span of a child born today. This is the result of a study done by the Ifo Institute for Economic Research, commissioned by the Bertelsmann Foundation. For this innovative study, the education economist Ludger Wößman calculated the adjusted earnings that result from education reform, which greatly reduces the number of so-called at-risk students. This way, for the first time, the long-term economic effects of education can be given a numeric value.

79. Bertelsmann Foundation, ed., *Chancen ermöglichen—Bildung stärken. Zur Lebenssituation sozial benachteiligter Kinder in Deutschland* (Creating Opportunities—Strengthening Education. On the Living Conditions of Socially Disad-

vantaged Children in Germany) (Gütersloh, 2009); Cornelia Stern, Christian Ebel, Veronika Schönstein, and Oliver Vorndran, eds., *Bildungsregionen gemeinsam gestalten. Erfahrung, Erfolge, Chancen* (Creating Educational Networks Together. Experiences, Successes, Opportunities) (Gütersloh, 2008); Jörg Dräger, "Bildung—unsere einzige Resource" (Education—Our Only Resource), in *Change,* special issue (Gütersloh, 2009), p. 49; and "Nachhaltigkeit durch Bildung" (Sustainablility Through Education), interview with Manfred Prenzel, pp. 40–45.

80. Bertelsmann, *Chancen ermöglichen—Bildung stärken.*

81. See the results of a labor market study by the Bertelsmann Foundation, Gütersloh, April 27, 2010. Temporary work in Germany has expanded greatly over the last decade and roughly doubled between 2000 and 2007. Nevertheless, in public opinion, this form of work still plays a secondary role. This is demonstrated in a study that compared typical employment models in international labor markets, conducted by the Bertelsmann Foundation in cooperation with the Institute for the Study of Labor. "New employment possibilities," wrote Dr. Gunter Thielen, chair of the Bertelsmann Foundation, in the study's introduction, "have been created through the easier use of temporary labor, which was made possible through labor market reforms. However, these possibilities seldom act as a bridge to regular employment." That is, an autonomous and permanent employment sector has developed consisting of workers whose hopes for a quick transition into regular employment have not been fulfilled. The seemingly permanent inequity between temporary and permanent employees does not comply with the basic tenets of a social market economy. The study *Atypical Employment and Low-Wage Work* compared additional atypical employment

relationships internationally, including part-time work, new forms of self-employment, and poorly paid labor.

82. Liz Mohn, Brigitte Mohn, Werner Weidenfeld, and Johannes Meier, eds., *Werte. Was die Gesellschaft zusammenhält* (Values. What Holds Society Together) (Gütersloh, 2007).

83. Michael Winterhoff, *Warum unsere Kinder Tyrannen werden. Oder: die Abschaffung der Kindheit* (Why Our Children Become Tyrants. Or, the Abolition of Childhood) (Gütersloh, 2008); Michael Winterhoff, *Tyrannen müssen nicht sein. Warum Erziehung allein nicht reicht—Auswege* (Tyrants Aren't Necessary. Why Rearing Children Is Not Enough—Ways Out) (Gütersloh, 2009).

84. At the end of October 2009, at the request of the Bertelsmann Foundation, TNS Emnid surveyed 1,003 German citizens.

85. Birgit Riess, ed., *Verantwortung für die Gesellschaft—verantwortlich für das Geschäft. Ein Management Handbuch* (Responsibility for Society—Responsible for the Company: A Handbook for Managers) (Gütersloh, 2006).

86. The figures for 2009 put Qatar and the United Arab Emirates among the top ten countries. Neither of them is a democracy. See Christian Welzel, *Ist Demokratie ein universell übertragbares Konzept? Erkenntnisse der empirischen Sozialforschung* (Is Democracy a Universally Transferable Concept? Findings from Empirical Social Research) (Bremen, 2007); and Bertelsmann Foundation, ed., *Bertelsmann Transformation Index 2008. Politische Gestaltung im internationalen Vergleich* (Bertelsmann Transformation Index. An International Comparison of Political Structures) (Gütersloh, 2008).

87. Ulrich Hemel, *Wert und Werte. Ethik für Manager—Ein Leitfaden für die Praxis* (Value and Values: Ethics for Managers—A Guideline for Practical Experience) (Munich, 2007), p. 320.

88. See www.bertelsmann-stiftung.de, focus area: Economy, and "Creating Corporate Social Responsibility (CSR)." See also Susanne Bergius, "Ethik an den Unis. Suche nach anständigem Verhalten" (Ethics at the Universities: The Search for Decent Behavior), *Frankfurter Rundschau,* Jan. 20, 2010.

89. Liz Mohn and Ursula von der Leyen, eds., *Familie gewinnt. Die Allianz und ihre Wirkung für Unternehmen und Gesellschaft* (Family Wins: The Alliance and Its Effect on Business and Society) (Gütersloh, 2007); and *Work-Life Balance. Meilensteine für eine zukunftsfähige Gesellschaft. Dokumentation zur Vereinbarkeit von Familie und Beruf im europäischen Vergleich* (Work-Life Balance: Milestones for a Sustainable Society. Documentation for a European Comparison of Compatibility of Family and Work) (Gütersloh, 2007).

90. Bertelsmann Foundation, ed., *Demographiemonitor, Bd. 1: Indikatoren-Katalog des demographischen Wandels; Bd. 2: Handlungsoptionen im demographischen Wandel* (Demographic Monitor, vol. 1: Catalogue of Indicators of Demographic Change; vol. 2, Options for Actions Within Demographic Change) (Gütersloh, 2006).

91. Youth Study 2006. The 15th Shell Youth Study is dedicated to the theme "Young and old: How does the young generation see itself—with all its expectations for its future— in an aging society?"

92. Urusla von der Leyen, "Der neue Weg—Familienpolitik" (The New Way—Family Politics), in L. Mohn and von der Leyen, *Familie gewinnt,* p. 9.

93. Werner Eichhorst, Lutz C. Kaiser, Eric Thode, and Verena Tobsch, *Vereinbarkeit von Familie und Beruf im internationalen Vergleich. Zwischen Paradigma und Praxis* (An International Comparison of the Reconciliation of Family and Work: Between Paradigm and Practice) (Gütersloh, 2008).

94. Christiane Flüter-Hoffman, *Familienfreundliche Regelungen in Tarifverträgen und Betriebsvereinbarungen. Beispiele guter Praxis* (Family-Friendly Regulations in Labor Contracts and Employment Agreements: Examples of Good Practices) (Cologne: Federal Ministry for Family Affairs, Senior Citizens, Women and Youth, 2005). See also L. Mohn and von der Leyen, *Familie gewinnt.*

95. See www.bertelsmann-stiftung.de, focus area: Family-Friendly Society. See also *Change. Das Magazin der Bertelsmann Stiftung* (Change: The Magazine of the Bertelsmann Foundation), March 2009.

96. See the Project of the Bertelsmann Foundation to Balance Work and Family Life. The foundation supports the Nuremberg region as it develops into a family-friendly economic region. The project partners are the Federal Ministry for Family Affairs, Senior Citizens, Women and Youth, associations, chambers, the working group for the reconciliation of family and work of the Initiative for Employment, and family alliances. The project duration was July 1, 2003, to June 30, 2011.

97. See www.bertelsmann-stiftung.de, focus area: Business Summer School: Business Women School, Berlin 2009. See also Kathrin Walther and Helga Lukoschat, *Kinder und Karrieren. Die neuen Paare* (Children and Careers: The New Couples), a study by the European Academy for Women in Politics and Economics, Berlin, commissioned by the Bertelsmann Foundation (Gütersloh, 2008); Martina Schraudner and Helga Lukoschat, *Gender als Innovationspotenzial in Forschung und Entwicklung* (Gender as Potential for Innovation in Research and Development) (Munich, 2006); *Work-Life-Balance für Führungskräfte* (Work-Life Balance for Management), a study by the EAF, appeared in "PERSONAL," July 2008.

98. Doreen Kimura, "Weibliches und männliches Gehirn" (Feminine and Masculine Brain), in Wolf Singer, ed., *Gehirn und Bewusstsein* (Brain and Consciousness) (Heidelberg/Berlin/Oxford, 1994), p. 78.

99. Berlin's former minister of justice Lore Maria Peschel-Gutzeit is a renowned expert on women's rights; in her political career, she worked to establish the legal equality of women. See Lore Maria Peschel-Gutzeit, *Die Auswirkung der Unterhaltsreform auf die Beratungspraxis* (The Effect of Alimony Reform on Consulting Practices) (Baden-Baden, 2008).

100. Bertelsmann Foundation, *Business Women School* (Berlin, 2009).

101. Yue-Sai Kan was born on October 1 in China. She is well known in China and in the United States and is especially respected for her humanitarian efforts. *People* magazine called her "the most famous woman in China."

102. An especially striking example of this problem is Thilo Sarrazin, *Deutschland schafft sich ab. Wie wir unser Land aufs Spiel setzen* (Germany Is Eradicating Itself: How We Are Risking Our Country) (Munich, 2010), and the debate that followed its publication.

103. See www.bertelsmann-stiftung.de, focus area: the Future of Integration. See also *Es ist Zeit für ein neues Miteinander. Neun Pfeiler der Integration. Ein "Manifest für Brückenbauer in Deutschland"* (It Is Time for a New Togetherness. Nine Pillars of Integration. A "Manifesto for Builders of Bridges in Germany") (Gütersloh, 2009).

104. Bertelsmann Foundation, ed., *Demokratie und Integration in Deutschland. Politische Führung und Partizipation aus Sicht von Menschen mit und ohne Migrationshintergrund* (Democracy and Integration in Germany: Political Leadership and Participation from the Points of View

of People with and Without a Migration Background) (Güter-sloh, 2009).

105. See www.bertelsmann-stiftung.de, focus area: Carl Bertelsmann Prize.

106. *Change. Integration durch Bildung. Das Magazin der Bertelsmann Stiftung* (Change: Integration Through Education: The Magazine of the Bertelsmann Foundation), Feb. 2008. The 1996 Carl Bertelsmann Prize had already been given to the Durham, Canada, Board of Education.

107. Bertelsmann Foundation, ed., *Die kulturellen Dimensionen des globalen Konfliktgeschehens. Kulturelle Konflikte im Zeitraum 1945–2007* (The Cultural Dimensions of Global Conflict: Cultural Conflicts in the Time Frame 1945–2007) (Gütersloh, 2009).

108. Huntington, *Clash of Civilizations.*

109. See www.bertelsmann-stiftung.de, project: Salzburg Trilogue.

110. Bertelsmann Foundation, *Voices for the Future: Global Crisis and the Human Potential: Trilogue Salzburg: 14–16 August 2009 in Salzburg, Austria.* A background paper by Surendra Munshi.

111. Jerome C. Glenn, Theodore J. Gordon, and Elizabeth Florescu, eds., *2009 State of the Future* (Washington, D.C.: The Millennium Project: World Federation of UN Associations, 2009).

112. Munshi background paper.

113. Bertelsmann Foundation, ed., *Managing the Crisis: A Comparative Analysis of Economic Governance in 14 Countries* (Gütersloh, 2010).

Insert Credits

Picture 1: Photograph: Veit Mette, Bielefeld

Picture 2: Teddy Kollek: Bertelsmann AG Archives

Picture 3: Bertelsmann Foundation

Picture 4: Photograph: Bernhard J. Holzner, Vienna

Picture 5: Bertelsmann Foundation Archives

Picture 6: Photograph: Veit Mette, Bielefeld

Picture 7: Photograph: Marc Darchinger, Berlin

Picture 8: Photograph: Benn Gabbe, PatrickMcMullan.com

Picture 9: Photograph: Thomas Kunsch, Bielefeld/
   Neubrandenburg

Picture 10: Photograph: Thomas Kunsch, Bielefeld/
   Neubrandenburg

Picture 11: Photograph: Thomas Kunsch, Bielefeld/
   Neubrandenburg

Picture 12: Frank Nürnberger, Berlin

Picture 13: Photograph: Thomas Kunsch, Bielefeld/
   Neubrandenburg

Picture 14: Bertelsmann AG Archives

Picture 15: Bertelsmann AG, Private Archives

Picture 16: Bertelsmann Foundation Archives

Picture 17: Photgraph: Arne Weychardt, Hamburg

Picture 18: German Stroke Aid Foundation/Bildschön Agency, Berlin

Picture 19: German Stroke Aid Foundation/Bildschön Agency, Berlin

Picture 20: Photograph: Thomas Kunsch, Bielefeld/ Neubrandenburg

Picture 21: Photograph: Thomas Kunsch, Bielefeld/ Neubrandenburg

Picture 22: Photograph: Veit Mette, Bielefeld

Index

Index

Index

About the Author

Following the death of her husband, Reinhard Mohn, Liz Mohn now represents the fifth generation of the ownership family Bertelsmann/Mohn. She is the vice chair of the Bertelsmann Foundation's executive board and of the board of trustees, and she is a supervisory board member of Bertelsmann AG. She is president of the German Stroke Aid Foundation, which she founded, chairwoman of the board of the Liz Mohn Foundation for Culture and Music, and chairwoman of the Curatorship of the Association of German Music Schools. In 1999, Liz Mohn became the first German woman to join the global think tank the Club of Rome.

About This Book

Liz Mohn and Andrea Stoll met during early conversations for a film about Reinhard Mohn, the husband of Liz Mohn. In 2008 they conducted a series of interviews, upon which this book is based.

Author Andrea Stoll has published several books and has written for numerous film projects. In addition, she worked as a professor of literature and screenwriting at the University of Salzburg from 1992 until 1997.